RESUME 101

HOW TO WRITE AN EFFECTIVE

RESUME,

LINKEDIN PROFILE,

AND COVER LETTER

STEVEN MOSTYN, MBA

REVIEWS

"Steven is the Resume Guru! His knowledge of resume ATS's algorithms helped me land a job in a very short time."
—*Aviva Nelkin, Executive Assistant*

"For anyone who wants the kind of resume that will get you noticed by both recruiters and hiring managers, I recommend Steven Mostyn's book."
—*Jermaine Mitchell, Sourcing Team Leader - Talent Acquisition at AdventHealth*

"As a consultant, my resume is my life's blood in getting my next engagement. Steven's resume increased my number of call backs, and I no longer worry about that next gig."
—*Patrick Welch, Independent Sr. Project Manager Consultant.*

"I was unemployed for over a year and frustrated until Steve's resume tips helped me land my next job."
—*Ryan Schmidt, Network Analyst*

"As a recruiter with over 20 years of experience, I can tell you Steven's custom resumes are the type of resumes recruiters and hiring managers will look at."
—*Sonja Gay, North America Recruiter at Willis Towers Watson*

RESUME 101

HOW TO WRITE AN EFFECTIVE RESUME, LINKEDIN PROFILE, AND COVER LETTER

STEVEN MOSTYN, MBA

Resume 101: How to Write an Effective Resume, LinkedIn Profile and Cover Letter
First Edition: 2020
ISBN: 978-0-9914900-0-4

This book is dedicated to my father, Murray,
and my son, Eli –
two of the most important people in my life.

CONTENTS

PREFACE

Why is this book needed?

Looking for a job is stressful. This is compounded when you don't know what you're doing – or if you're doing it right.

Most job seekers are never taught how to create an effective resume, cover letter, or LinkedIn profile. They go their entire careers without having learned how to properly create these tools. The result? Failure and frustration.

It doesn't have to be that way.

In my 20+ years of experience as a resume expert at Elite Pro Resume Services and as a recruiter for some of North America's largest companies, I have helped over 1,000 people land jobs in various professions. This includes new grads looking for their first job, CEOs in established careers, and many who were unemployed and had given up all hope of finding a job.

There's a real need to educate the job-seeking audience. To meet this need, I wrote *Resume 101: How to Write an Effective Resume, LinkedIn Profile and Cover Letter*. This comprehensive, step-by-step guide will help you develop essential job-seeking skills.

Resume 101 was written with the busy job seeker in mind. The writing is clear, the format is simple, and the chapters are brief and straightforward. To get the most out of this book, read it more than once. Apply what you learn. When you do, you'll have the job-search skills you need to find your dream job.

Read on and start your journey to success.

1

NEVER GIVE UP

Looking for a job is one of the most stressful life experiences. The feeling of having no control over your employment situation and not knowing how things are going to turn out can be frightening.

Has your life's path unexpectedly veered? It could be that you've found yourself suddenly unemployed. Maybe you were fired from your last job and have been unemployed for months. Or perhaps you are a recent college grad and have seen all your friends land jobs while you are still stuck at home. No matter what your own circumstances are, don't give up. Be positive.

You might be thinking, "It's easy to tell someone to be positive, but it's another thing to be positive when you're down."

That's true. But despite your present difficulties, you owe it to yourself to move forward and turn over a new leaf.

In any pursuit, an individual will face multiple obstacles and failures. Often, the difference between success and failure is that, despite obstacles, a successful person never gives up. To truly be successful, an individual must taste some form of failure and move on to greater heights.

When looking for a job, expect to encounter many ups

and downs. A potential employer might not respond to your application. Or, after what you thought was a great interview, you are rejected by an employer. These things happen to all of us.

To land your dream job, you must never give up, even in the face of adversity.

WHAT DO THESE 10 FAMOUS INDIVIDUALS HAVE IN COMMON?

1. Abraham Lincoln
2. Albert Einstein
3. Colonel Sanders
4. Dr. Seuss
5. J.K. Rowling
6. Oprah Winfrey
7. Steve Jobs
8. Sylvester Stallone
9. Walt Disney
10. Winston Churchill

Although they all faced rejection in pursuit of their dreams, they never gave up – and they all rose to the top of their professions!

Abraham Lincoln had a multitude of failures in his life, including losing major elections, failing in business, and having a nervous breakdown. Despite these setbacks, Lincoln went on to become one of the greatest presidents in the history of the United States.

Albert Einstein was told by his teachers that he would never amount to anything. Einstein is now considered to be one of the greatest physicists who ever lived.

Colonel Sanders failed at many endeavors until, at age 65, he started KFC , one of the world's largest fast food chains.

Dr. Seuss was rejected multiple times before his first book was accepted for publication. Today, he is one of the most beloved children's authors of all time.

J.K. Rowling was dirt poor and had been rejected by most publishers before her first Harry Potter novel was finally accepted. Her books are now consistent best sellers.

Oprah Winfrey was told by one of her first bosses that she was too emotional for television. She went on to become a famous television host and a household name.

Steve Jobs was fired from his own company and was considered finished. He made a huge comeback and was rehired by Apple, helping transform the company into one of the most successful businesses in the world.

Sylvester Stallone was struggling as an actor before he wrote and starred in Rocky. He ended up winning an Oscar and went on to star in many other blockbusters.

Walt Disney was fired from his newspaper job for having a lack of imagination. He went on to create the famous and beloved Disney animation studio.

Winston Churchill was one of the greatest wartime leaders and a World War II hero. Prior to this success, Churchill failed so badly during World War I that he was dismissed from his political party for incompetence.

MY OWN STORY

I am not just preaching to the choir about adversity. In my

own life, I have weathered many ups and downs.

My parents were told by my second-grade teacher that I would never amount to anything due to my extreme hyperactivity. Despite these early academic challenges, I wound up winning a scholarship for my undergraduate degree and obtained my MBA with a perfect 4.0 grade point average.

Before becoming an expert in job hunting and recruiting, I struggled to find employment. In my early twenties, I was unemployed for almost a year. When I wanted to get into the recruitment field, I was rejected by many companies. I never gave up and eventually landed my first job. Almost 20 years later, I've become one of the leading experts in job search and recruitment and have even written two best-selling books on the topic, *Recruiting 101: The Fundamentals of Being a Great Recruiter* and *Job Search: Fundamentals of Effective Job Hunting, Resumes and Interviews.*

In my career, I have had my share of struggles. At my first job, I was told by the vice president of recruitment that the managers made a mistake by hiring me. He said I did not have the right personality to be a successful recruiter. Instead of being discouraged, I was motivated to work harder. At that job, I wound up being the top rookie recruiter; soon afterward, the VP who said I would not make it was out of the business.

Sometimes things turn out differently than expected. At my first corporate recruitment leadership job, the senior VP told me she wanted to fire me in my first week due to my unique and progressive style. After I produced exceptional results, she became one of my biggest supporters.

Looking back, I wish I could have told the younger me that everything would turn out great and that I would reach the top of my profession and become a two-time bestselling author, but that is not how life works. During our struggles, we often do not see the whole picture. Today's pain is tomorrow's badge of courage.

Now, having gone through the struggle and climbed to the top, I've learned the key to success. How did I do it? I never gave up. I stayed positive.

HOW TO STAY POSITIVE

Here are 10 great ways to stay positive:

1. Dwell on the positive and not the negative. Every day, list all the positive things you have done.
2. Try to only associate with positive people. Negative people only bring you down, so keep in the company of positive people.
3. Read inspirational books, quotes, and articles. Watch inspirational movies.
4. Think of mistakes as learning experiences. Don't dwell on them.
5. Keep track of your successes. Whenever you feel down, look at your successes as a reminder of what you have done.
6. Whenever you have negative thoughts, have a mentor or friend you trust motivate you to turn those negative thoughts around.
7. Learn how to accept change and adapt to it. In life, there are many things outside of our control. What we can't control, we must accept.
8. Do not take failure and criticism to heart. Move from being a victim to being a survivor who triumphs over adversity.

9. Focus on what you currently have, not on what you do not have.
10. Visualize a positive future and all its endless possibilities.

A NEGATIVE ATTITUDE CAN PREVENT YOU FROM GETTING HIRED!

Don't let your frustration with your current situation show when you are looking for a job. When meeting with a potential employer, how you portray yourself could impact whether or not you land the job. If you come across as angry and frustrated, potential employers will view you as an angry and frustrated person and will not be interested in hiring you. Most people want to be around positive and upbeat individuals, and that includes potential employers. You owe it to yourself to learn how to project a positive attitude despite your frustration.

CONCLUSION

Even if you are not at a good place in your career, stay positive. The long road to success may start at the lowest level, but it ends up at the greatest heights. Never accept failure and don't take criticism to heart. Instead of being frustrated and depressed by failures, use these setbacks to motivate yourself to move forward.

Don't give up. Stay positive. By learning this skill, you will find many employers will be more inclined to consider you as a job candidate.

2

CREATING AN EFFECTIVE RESUME

When looking for a job, your resume is the most important marketing tool at your disposal.

They say there is nothing like first impressions, and this is so true when a potential employer reads your resume. It is their first interaction with you.

A recruiter or hiring manager will make a split-second decision about you based on your resume. Your resume will be put in the wastebasket if it does not stand out, isn't formatted properly, doesn't have correct spelling and grammar, or if your skills are not clearly identified.

This chapter will take you step-by-step through the essential parts of creating a resume:

1. Ideal resume length
2. Proper resume format
3. Font, color, and other aesthetics
4. Honesty and integrity
5. Spelling, grammar, and writing style
6. Complying with resume norms
7. Job titles

8. Key sections of a resume
9. Section placement
10. Additional resume sections
11. Customizing your resume

(Please note: The names, contact info, and company names used in this are fictional.)

PART 1 - RESUME LENGTH

The question for many job hunters is "How long should my resume be?" For individuals with five years of experience or less, the rule of thumb is to keep a resume to one full page. For those with over five years of experience (not including executives and those who have specialized talent, such as academics and scientific researchers), a resume should be no longer than two pages. For executives and those with specialized talent, a resume can be over three pages.

The reason you limit resume size is that HR and hiring managers do not have the time to read long resumes. The average recruiter today has about 55 jobs they work on at any given time and about 55 applicants for each of these roles. If you do the math, you'll see there is no way they have time to read a long resume.

PART 2 - RESUME FORMAT

When formatting a resume, the recommendation is to use a standard Word document or a PDF file in a version that most employers will have. Try not to use uncommon or unfamiliar file formats, such as JPEG. Why? You want to ensure that your file can be opened without any difficulty. If a hiring manager cannot open your file, it will be game over for you.

PART 3 - FONT, COLOR, AND OTHER AESTHETICS

Use a standard Word font like Arial, Calibri, or Times New Roman. These are standard business fonts and you should stick with one of them. The font should be consistent throughout the entire resume. Keep it to a size 12 – not too small to read but not so big as to overpower the page.

No matter how much you are tempted, keep the font color plain black. The only time you should deviate from this would be if you were applying for an art-related job – then your artistic creativity can trump standard formats.

You want your resume to stand out. But at the same time, you don't want it to be so different that it attracts negative attention. Bolding and highlighting is a good way to draw potential employers' eyes to areas you want them to notice. Bolding key topics, such as Job History or Education, is recommended. Bold and/or underline important words like job titles. By bolding and highlighting key areas and words, your resume will stand out but will not deviate from the accepted formats.

PART 4 - HONESTY AND INTEGRITY

Your resume should honestly reflect your true skills. This is paramount.

If your resume is embellished, at some stage in the hiring

process – likely the interview stage – you will be caught. An interviewer will ask you questions about the skills or experience you listed, and you won't be able to answer. If your resume lists job titles you never held, companies you have not worked at, education you do not possess, or falsified job dates, these things will be flagged during a background check.

Many employers use third-party background check companies. Employers listed on your resume and educational institutions you attended will be contacted directly during the background check. If what you listed on your resume cannot be verified, you will be disqualified from that job, even if you've made it up to the offer stage.

It is okay to list things on your resume that you have done but are not an expert in. But you should never lie outright.

PART 5 - SPELLING, GRAMMAR, AND WRITING STYLE

An unprofessional resume full of spelling and grammatical errors will negatively impact your ability to get a job. Your candidacy for a job depends on a cleanly written resume.

Even if you are talented in your field, many hiring managers and recruiters will deem you incompetent if you do not use proper English. It is important and worth the time it takes to make sure your resume is free of errors. If you are not the world's best speller or your grammar could use some brushing up, ask friends and family for help. Beware: Most automated spell checks do not effectively fix all errors, so don't depend on your spell check.

In terms of writing style, always write in the third person on resumes. Writing in the first person is considered unprofessional.

You should write using professional words and technical terms; slang is not acceptable.

PART 6 - COMPLYING WITH RESUME NORMS

What is considered normal resume content in some countries is unacceptable in others. For example, in North America, including a photo of your family in your resume is a no-no. So is including how many people are in your family, their names, ages, etc. Putting these items on your resume will make you look strange compared to other job seekers and could cost you the job.

Learn the resume norms of the country you're currently living in and comply with them. A new issue I see with some job seekers is to use abbreviated short form resume that has more graphics than content. My recommendation is this: until the majority of job seekers in your location and profession use this format, do not use this type of resume. Stick with a more traditional format.

PART 7 - JOB TITLES

When looking at resumes, the first thing many recruiters look at is job titles. This is why you need to create effective job titles. Below are some key tips.

- Your job title must be the most common title, one that is recognizable by most employers. You should use common vernacular if your title is not easily recognizable. For example, if your title is just Consultant, no one will know what kind of consultant you are, so you should make your job title more specific: Project Manager - Consultant. If your company uses an odd title for your job, you should still put your legal title in brackets or with a dash, followed by the commonly recognized title. Do this so it can be matched to your employee records at the background check stage. An example might be having a title such as business consultant for an account manager. You might replace this with Account Manager – Business Consultant.

- Always be honest with job titles. Although you can change your title to the most common version, you should not embellish it. For example, if you are an accountant but not an accounting manager, it would be misleading to have Accountant Manager as your title. Dishonesty will come back to haunt you on many background checks.

- Keep your titles as short as possible, but include as much searchable information as you can. From an SEO (search engine optimization) perspective, long titles are harder to find and clog up SEO algorithms. At the same time, job titles must be optimized with enough information so that hiring managers will find your resume on databases, job boards, and the web.

- Words that are searched together should be placed together in the job title. For example, many health care recruiters search ICU & RN together, so these words should be placed together in the job title.

- Secondary search words are a good idea to add to your job title. For example, in technology, some recruiters search for Java or J2EE, so having Java / J2EE Developer as a title will increase the chances of that resume showing up in their search.

Examples of Titles in Different Industries:

Accounting
Chartered Accountant / Auditor

Engineering
Mechanical Engineer / Engineering

Financial Services
Financial Planner / Advisor

Healthcare
ICU RN / Registered Nurse Intensive Care Unit

Insurance
Life Insurance Advisor / Agent

Manufacturing
Plant Manager / Superintendent

Oil & Gas
Field Operator / Oil & Gas

Pharmaceutical
Pharmaceutical Sales Representative / Account Manager

Retail
Retail Store Manager

Technology
J2EE / Java Developer

PART 8 - KEY SECTIONS OF A RESUME

The main sections of your resume are:
1. Your Personal Info
2. Objective
3. Education
4. Job History
5. Skills

Below you will find a description of each.

1. YOUR PERSONAL INFO

This section appears at the top of a resume and includes your basic information. Some job seekers are afraid to include their personal contact details and address. This is a mistake; it makes it harder for employers to contact you.

If you have a major certification or education in the profession you are applying for, I would recommend you put it beside your name. Also, your name should be shown in the largest font on the resume. If you used 12 for your resume, your name should be set at 14. Example of a personal info section:

Jane Smith CFP

534 Jackson St • Plano, Texas • 75027
Tel: (111) 111-1111   Email: name@gmail.com

2. OBJECTIVE

There are some experts who believe you should not include the objective section in your resume, calling it a waste of valuable resume real estate. But many employers expect to see an objective section, so I would still recommend having it on your resume. Stating your objective serves is an introduction to your resume. Keep this section brief. It should highlight your background in one or two sentences.

Example of an Objective section:

*Future-focused **Financial Analyst** with a commitment to quality and accuracy seeks a progressive role with a dynamic, growth-oriented organization where financial modeling and analytical techniques can be leveraged to achieve exceptional results.*

3. EDUCATION SECTION

This self-explanatory section focuses on your education, certifications, and courses. You should include education, certifications, and courses that are relevant to the job you're searching for. If you have certifications that are not relevant to the job you want, do not list them on your resume. For example, if you have a personal training certification but are not looking to get hired as a personal trainer, that certification doesn't need to be on your resume.

You can also list courses in progress or ones you are looking to do in the future. This will show initiative on your part and might give you an advantage over other candidates. Another good reason to include courses and certifications is that if a recruiter searches for a specific credential, you might pop up in their search.

Where should the education section be placed in your resume? If you are applying for a job where specific education and/or certification is critical, place it near the top. If not, place it at the bottom.

If you are experienced in your field, you might choose to leave out the year you graduated.

Academic achievements, such as high GPAs or scholarships, should be included in this section. Many entry-level roles like to see potential candidates' GPAs.

Example of an Education section:

EDUCATION

Formal Education:

MBA – Focus in Financial Modeling (4.0 GPA)
University of Florida   2017

Bachelor of History
York University, Toronto   2015

Professional Certifications:

PMP - Certified Project Manager
Project Management Institute   2016

Lean Six Sigma Green Belt - In Progress

4. JOB HISTORY SECTION

The job history section is the most important section on your resume. It is the section which describes your work history. It is also the section hiring managers are going to focus on.

Your jobs should be listed in chronological order, from newest to oldest. Your company, job title, employment duration, and city you worked in should all be listed before your experience. It is a good idea to write a synopsis of the company you worked at. In bullet points, note your positive experiences in that job, from most important to the least important. This is a way to market yourself to employers: they see what you have achieved and how you can help them. Be sure to include any large-scale achievements you had at that job.

For the tech sector, list the technical environment and specific skills you used at the end of the position.

Example of a Job History section:

WORK EXPERIENCE

Health System America
Director Talent Acquisition, Seattle Washington
(November 2013 - Present)

Health System America is one of the largest health care organizations in the US, with more than 100,000 employees across the country. The system supports 80 hospitals as well as 100 long term acute care facilities. As a director of talent acquisition, I led the talent acquisition functions for the entire organization. Specific duties include:

- Built Health System America's talent acquisition department from scratch, including hiring the recruitment team; creating metrics, processes, and SLAs, and defining overall strategy.
- Saved the organization 50 million dollars in agency saving over a 5 year period
- Reduced time to fill metrics from over 50 days to 28 days
- Led, trained, mentored and guided a team of 50+, including 5 managers, 30 recruiters, 10 sourcers and 10 onboarding specialists.
- Designed, developed, and implemented recruitment process improvements.

Successful large-scale projects: Staffed new units for Operating Room, CVICU, Free-standing ER, Dialysis, Peds, NICU, ICU, Med-Surg and Wellness Center.

5. SKILLS SECTION

The skills section is the area of the resume where you list all your relevant skills. This area is also important in terms of

SEO – when filling a job, the keywords that recruiters search for are often the skills you list.

To pop up in a recruiter's search, make your skills specific. For example, don't just list MS Office as a skill; include the specific Office programs that you are familiar with: Word, Excel, etc. Sometimes the smallest skill can lead you to pop up in a recruiter's search.

Example of Skills Section:

SKILLS

• Microsoft Office (Word, Excel, PowerPoint) • Accounting & Payroll Systems (ADP, JD Edwards, Oracle) • Financial Statements • Accounts Payable/Receivable • Tax Reporting • Bank Reconciliation • General Ledgers • Payroll • Profit and Loss Analysis

In occupations where education or skills are critical, you could put education and/or skills directly after the objective section.

PART 9 - WHERE TO PLACE THOSE SECTIONS ON A RESUME

In most cases, your resume should follow this order:

1. Personal info
2. Objective
3. Job history
4. Education
5. Skills

In occupations where education or skills are critical, you could put education and/or skills directly after the Objective section.

PART 10 - ADDITIONAL RESUME SECTIONS & WHEN TO ADD THEM TO YOUR RESUME

Some job hunters put additional sections in their resumes. For each of these sections, the pros and cons will be discussed as well as when to use them. These sections include:

- **Unpaid Internships/Co-Ops** – Only list unpaid internship or co-op experience if it is relevant to your field or if you are lacking real-world job experience.
- **Volunteer Experience** – Include your volunteer experience if you are applying to jobs that look fondly on volunteering, like non-profits or social-minded companies. Also, many entry-level jobs like to see what you have done (other than school and work), so this could be useful for these jobs. Volunteer experience could also be used to fill a void, i.e. for individuals with limited work experience or who have been out of work for a while.
- **Hobbies and Interests** – For the most part, this section is not needed unless you know a potential employer values specific hobbies and interests.
- **Awards and Achievements** – This section can be useful if you have achieved certain job-related achievements in your profession, such as winning industry awards.
- **Industry Experiences** – This optional section is where you list the industries you have worked in. This section

is good for candidates who work in consulting or are looking to get into it.

- **Patents and Publications** – This is a rare section, usually reserved for very technical roles. In some engineering roles, this section is quite useful.
- **Languages** – This section lists the languages you speak. In certain countries – like Canada, where both English and French are spoken – speaking more than one language can increase your chances of getting the job. Do your homework to see if employers in your geographical area are interested in multi-lingual candidates.

PART 11 – CUSTOMIZE YOUR RESUME TO THE JOB YOU ARE APPLYING FOR

Unless you are using a Quick Apply feature, you should customize your resume for every job you apply for. This means that for every application, you should customize your resume with keywords you see in that particular job description.

CONCLUSION

In Chapter 4, you will be given examples of resume templates that use the above tips.

3

THE IMPORTANCE OF SEO AND ATS SYSTEMS

Search engine optimization, or SEO, is a method used to increase website visitors by ranking the site higher in search engine results. In terms of job search, SEO is one of the techniques used by job hunters to get their resumes and other online profiles at the top of recruiters' and hiring managers' search lists.

Applicant tracking systems (ATS) are where companies post jobs and where candidates can apply for jobs. This is also where companies store candidates' information. ATS systems are important for job seekers because the system can reject your job application if you do not use the right keywords (SEO).

This chapter will teach you how to use SEO to get your resume and profile past ATS checkpoints and to the top of recruiters' inboxes.

Note: some of the points in this chapter will be a review of what we covered in the last chapter.

PART 1: CHOOSE THE RIGHT LOCATIONS FOR YOUR PROFILES

This might sound basic, but when you are setting up your resume on resume databases and creating online profiles, make sure you always put yourself in the right location. When a recruiter searches for profiles, they usually search by location, such as ZIP/postal code, city, and/or state. If you choose the wrong location, you will not pop up in the correct recruiter's search.

An SEO technique you can try is to choose larger city centers near where you live (as opposed to smaller suburbs and outlying towns). Recruiters tend to search in bigger markets, so your best bet is to list your profiles in nearby population centers.

PART 2: KEYWORDS

Adding keywords to your resume and online profiles can propel you to the top of a recruiter's list.

When recruiters search for a profile online or through a database, many of them use keywords given to them by hiring managers. If the keywords they're searching by are not on your resume, you will not pop up in their search.

Increase your chances by adding relevant keywords to the Skills and Work History sections of your resume. Try to think of the most common skills in your profession. For example, an Accounts Payable professional might add these keywords: Reconciliation, Financial Statements, Accounts Payable/Receivable, Tax Reporting, General Ledgers, Profit and Loss, and Accounting.

Another tip is to look at job descriptions for jobs similar to the one you want, find words that are commonly used, and add them to your resume and online profiles.

PART 3: JOB TITLES

When looking at resumes and profiles, the #1 thing recruiters search for is job titles. This is why you need an effective job title. Below are tips to increase the SEO of your job titles.

- Your job title must be the most common title, one that is recognizable by most employers. If your job title is not a common title for your area of expertise, recruiters may not find your resume or profile. Go to the major job websites to find the most common title for your job.
- Keep your title(s) as short as possible, but include as much searchable information as you can. From an SEO perspective, long titles are harder to find and clog up SEO algorithms. At the same time, job titles must be optimized with enough information so that hiring managers will find your resume.
- Words that are searched together should be placed together in the job title. For example, many recruiters search for ICU and RN together, so these words should be placed together in the job title.
- Secondary search words are a good idea to add to your job title. For example, a programmer could put Java/J2EE Developer as their job title so that their profile will pop up when recruiters search for Java or J2EE.

PART 4: STRATEGICALLY INJECTING YOUR JOB TITLE IN YOUR RESUME AND PROFILE

Strategically placing your job title multiple times in your resume and profiles can increase its SEO and make it rank higher in recruiters' searches. SEO increases every time a keyword is placed in a resume or online profile, so insert your job title throughout your resume without destroying its flow or ruining proper sentence structure. Great places to add your job title are the Objective, Work Experience, and Skills sections.

PART 5: THE POWER OF REFRESHING YOUR RESUME ON ONLINE JOB BOARDS

Another way to increase your SEO is to periodically refresh your resume and online profiles. On many job boards, recently added or recently updated profiles are ranked higher in a search. Instead of starting all over again to get a higher ranking, simply updating and making small changes to your resume/profile will refresh your it and bring you to the top of recruiters' search lists.

CONCLUSION

By improving your resume's SEO, you will increase the chances that your resume and online profiles appear higher on recruiters' lists when they search for candidates. It will also decrease the chances of your application being rejected by ATS systems.

4

EXAMPLES OF
RESUME TEMPLATES

This chapter will bring together all you learned in Chapters 2 and 3 and show five sample resumes. These cover five different industries and five levels of experience, including:

1. Pharmaceutical account manager with less than 5 years of experience
2. Entry level HR
3. Experienced software developer
4. Executive
5. Unemployed Accounts Payable

Explanations are given above each template, highlighting things in the resume that you can implement.

Please note: These resume templates are meant to be guides for you to use and customize for your own profession. Listing every potential profession and career stage in one book is impossible.

RESUME TEMPLATE 1

This is a sample resume for someone with several years' experience in the pharmaceutical field; this person is looking for a sales job in that field. Note that the seeker uses keywords and emphasizes sales accomplishments by mentioning the targets he met. Also, different words for sales are woven into the resume to improve SEO.

Fred Smith

111 Hook St • Plano, Texas • 75027

Tel: (111) 111-1111   Email: name@gmail.com

Future-focused **Account Manager** with a proven track record of hitting numbers seeks a dynamic, growth-oriented organization in the pharmaceutical industry where innovative sales skills can be leveraged to achieve exceptional results.

WORK EXPERIENCE

Pharmaceuticals R'US
Account Manager, Plano Texas   (November 2017 - Present)
Pharmaceuticals R'US is one of the US's largest wholesale drug companies, with over 10,000 employees and market distribution in all 50 states. As an account manager, I developed new business for the Southwest division. Specific duties and accomplishments include:
- Hit 120% of sales quota by producing over 10 million dollars in revenue.
- Top 10 account manager in the company for Revenue Quota in 2017
- Successfully developed new business by landing 12 major accounts.
- Executed creative business development techniques to define and develop potential new customers within the specialty wholesale pharmacy market.
- Made 2017 Sales Club

Pharma-Club
Account Manager, Plano Texas   (April 2015- November 2017)
Pharma-Club is one of the fastest growing wholesale drug companies in the United States. As an account manager, I developed new business for the West division. Specific duties and accomplishments included:
- Hit 100% of sales quota by producing over 5 million dollars in revenue.
- Top rookie account manager.
- Successfully developed new business by landing 5 major accounts.
- Executed creative business development techniques to define and develop potential new customers within the specialty wholesale pharmacy market.

EDUCATION

Bachelor of Commerce - University of Texas   2017

SKILLS

Microsoft Office (Word, Excel, PowerPoint) • Salesforce • CRM • Pharmaceutical Sales

RESUME TEMPLATE 2

This resume is an example of a recent HR graduate looking for her first HR job. Her internship in HR is listed first, followed by an unrelated part-time job that shows more work history. A minor HR function is described in the part-time job, demonstrating more HR experience. HR courses are listed in the Education section, proving the applicant has at least academic experience with HR. Her GPA is listed because many employers look at GPA for new grads. In the Skills section, all academic and internship experiences are listed. An in-progress HR certification is included in case that term is searched; it also shows initiative. Finally, the keywords "HR" and "Human Resources" are woven repeatedly into the resume to improve SEO.

Jane Smith
111 Hook St • Denver, Colorado • 80022

Tel: (111) 111-1111

Email: name@gmail.com

Future-focused recent **HR** graduate seeks a dynamic, growth-oriented entry level Human Resources position where exceptional customer service skills can be used to improve HR departments.

WORK EXPERIENCE

Bus Depot
HR intern, Denver Colorado   (March 2017 – May 2017)

Bus Depot is the leading manufacturer of bus parts in the world. As an HR intern, I performed human resources generalist functions. Specific duties included:
- Processed and analyzed HR benefit documents to ensure they were compliant.
- Onboarded all new employees, ensuring they received great customer service from HR.
- Analyzed and uploaded HR documents into the HRIS, PeopleSoft, and Taleo systems.
- Created Excel spreadsheets and PowerPoint human resources projects for HR leaders.
- Screened and performed HR behavior interviews to determine candidates' fit.

Sunglasses Emporium
Sales Representative – Part-Time   (February 2016 - Present)

Sunglasses Emporium is a niche retail store that sells sunglasses and custom beachwear. Specific duties included:
- Provided exceptional customer service to shoppers by offering custom solutions.
- Answered questions related to products.
- Sold customers products based on what they were looking for.
- Performed minor HR functions by interviewing and screening potential new staff.

EDUCATION

Bachelor of Human Resources Management – Rutgers University (3.2 GPA)   2018
Courses: HR Policies, Recruiting, Benefits, Employee Relations, Compensation, HRIS

SHRM Certification   In Process

SKILLS

Microsoft Office (Word, Excel, PowerPoint) • HR Policies • HRIS • PeopleSoft • Taleo • Benefits
HR Onboarding • Recruiting • Interviewing • Employee Relations • Compensation

RESUME TEMPLATE 3

This is the resume of a senior technical software developer with J2EE/Java experience. For the job title, both Java and J2EE are listed in case either of them pop up on a search. Technical skills are included after each role to show technical environment and increase SEO. The Experience section is detailed, but it's written so that non-technical people can understand the basic concepts. Longer technical skills are listed in the Skills section in case they pop up in a search. The candidate's master's degree is listed beside his name, putting emphasis on his educational achievement. The job title is used multiple times in the resume to improve SEO.

Jeff Smith, MCS
111 Hook St • San Jose, California • 95108

Tel: (111) 111-1111

Email: name@gmail.com

Results-oriented **Senior Java Software Developer** with a proven track record of delivering sofware solutions in the financial industry seeks a dynamic, growth-oriented organization where exceptional software development skills can be leveraged to achieve outstanding results.

EDUCATION

Formal Education:

Master of Computer Science – California Institute of Technology	2010
Bachelor of Computer Science – California Institute of Technology	2008

Professional Certifications:

Oracle Certified Master Developer	2016
Oracle Certified Master Java EE 5 Enterprise Architect	In Process

WORK EXPERIENCE

Financial-ecom Inc

Senior Java/J2EE Software Developer, San Jose California   (March 2014 – present)

Financial-ecom Inc is a software development company that creates mobile solutions for the financial services sector. As a senior Java software developer, I analyzed, designed and developed mobile software solutions for the financial industry. Specific duties included:

- Involvement in various phases of Software Development Life Cycle (SDLC) such as requirements gathering, modeling, analysis, design, development and testing.
- Designed and developed various modules of the applications with J2EE design architecture, using eAgent framework JSPs, HTML, AJAX, JQuery, iFrame and JavaScript.
- Designed and implemented a Node.js-based mobile text and voice messaging app and its cloud backend.
- Developed browser-based application for mobile and desktop using Custom Solutions.
- Used J2EE design patterns like Factory, Application Service, Business Delegate, Service Locator, View Helper, Cojmposite View, MVC and DAO to implement business tier using sessions beans.
- Deployed the application in WebSphere Application Server 6.0.1 and Configured JMS in the WebSphere application server to send messages in the queue.

Environment: Java, J2EE, Servlets, Spring Boot, Spring Dependency Injection (DI), Spring MVC, Apache Kafke, XML, REST Web Services, HTML5, CSS3, UML Diagrams, Data Services, JDBC, Git, JUNIT, Maven, JavaScript, JSON, Logback, PL/SQL, JAX-RS, OOAD, Scrum, IBM Rational Rose, WebSphere, JSPs, Node.js, AJAX, JQuery, iFrame, JavaScript.

WORK EXPERIENCE - CONTINUED

Trading Floor Software Solutions
Java/J2EE Software Developer, San Jose California   (April 2008 – March 2014)

Trading Floor Software Solutions is a software development company that creates trading floor software for the financial services industry. As a Java software developer, I analyzed, designed and developed mobile software solutions for the financial industry. Specific duties included:

- Involved in various phases of Software Development Life Cycle (SDLC) such as requirements gathering, modeling, analysis, design, development and testing.
- Designed and developed the messaging framework for communication between Workflow Manager and other enterprise applications over XML and MQ-Series using J2EE.
- Wrote complex SQLs for creating, retrieving, updating and deleting data in Oracle database.
- Development involving design, implementation and coding in Perl, XML, Java, Java Servlets, J2EE, EJB, JSP, etc.

Environment: Java, J2EE, Spring, Struts, iBATIS, JSP, AJAX, HTML, Tomcat 6.0, Oracle 12g, Maven, Log4J, slf4j, iText, Edit Plus, Eclipse IDE, JUnit, WinCVS, Axis2, JSON, WSDL, Web Services, Win Merge, TOAD.

SKILLS

Languages: Java, C/C++UNIX Shell, SQL, PL/SQL
Technologies: JSP, Servlets, JNDI, JDBC, EJB, JMS, JSF, Java Beans, SOP, JAXP, AJAX, AWT, Swings, CSS, ILOG, JXPath, Xpath
Web Technologies: HTML, DHTML, XML, CSS, JavaScript
Distributed Technologies: RMI, EJB, JMS, Data Warehouse
Application Server: JBoss, Apache Tomcat 5.5/6.0, IBM Websphere
J2EE Frameworks: Struts, Spring, ANT build tool, Log4J, MVC, Hibernate, IDE's Eclipse, RAD, IntelliJ
Databases: Oracle, MS Access, DB2 UDB, MySQL
Version Control Tools: Rational ClearCase, WinCVS, RequisitePro, ClearQuest, SVN
Testing Tools: JUnit, Win Runner
Case Tools: Rational Rose, UML, OOAD, RUP
Operating Systems: Windows 8/7/XP/MS-DOS, UNIX

AWARDS/PATENTS/PUBLICATIONS

- 2014 - Developer of the Year, Developers Association of America
- US Patent - #114,574,812,456, ABCD – Mobile Transference
- US Patent - #114,574,812,456, DCBE – Trading Transference
- Smith, J. (03.16.2016) "Case Study in Mobile Transference". Java Publications Inc. Volume 37.

RESUME TEMPLATE 4

This resume is an example of a health care executive looking for a job as a COO. Her RN and MBA credentials are listed beside her name to emphasize her health care and educational background. In this resume, the Skills section comes before Experience to emphasize keywords that are not only searchable but demonstrate her executive leadership. Listed throughout the resume are achievements in each role. Earlier roles are downplayed; more emphasis is given to her leadership roles. Finally, the job title repeatedly used throughout, to improve SEO.

Stephanie Smith, RN, MBA
111 Hook St • New York, New York • 10009

Tel: (111) 111-1111

Email: name@gmail.com

A recognized transformational **Chief Operating Officer COO** leader in healthcare with over 30 years of progressive experience turning around unprofitable hospitals seeks a growth opportunity with a dynamic, growth-oriented organization.

EXECUTIVE SKILLS

Strategic Business Transformation • Lean Process Improvements • Compliance
Leading and Managing People • Operations • Six Sigma • Cost Reductions • Project Management
Microsoft Office (Word, Excel, PowerPoint, Project) • Builder • Resource Forecasting
Strategic Planning • Analytics • Negotiations • Turnaround Strategy Business Optimization

WORK EXPERIENCE

Hospital of the Bronx
COO/Chief Operation Officer, Bronx, New York   (March 2014 – present)

With over 1,000 beds, Hospital of the Bronx is one of the largest hospitals in New York state and services over 100,000 patients every year. As the COO/Chief Operating Officer, I turned around the hospital's operations. Specific duties included:

- Led the development and implementation of an organizational turnaround strategy, as well as management of cost-reduction solutions (OR, ER, ICU and Environmental Services) which resulted in the saving of over 300 million dollars in less than 4 years.
- Managed a large team of 10 direct reports and over 1,000 indirect reports.
- Helped ensure the hospital passed all major Hospital Compliance Acts, such as the Joint Commission.
- Redesigned the organization's performance improvement processes, which resulted in significant advancement in leadership accountability and organizational operations.
- Through improvements in nursing operations, helped the hospital obtain and maintain Magnet Status designation.

Hospital of the Burroughs
COO/Chief Operation Officer, Long Island, New York   (March 2010 – March 2014)

Hospital of the Burroughs is the largest hospital on Long Island with over 500 beds and services over 50,000 patients every year. As the COO/Chief Operating Officer, I turned around the hospital's operations. Specific duties included:

- Led the development and implementation of an organizational turnaround strategy of cost-reduction solutions in Med-surg and OR, which resulted in over 600 million dollars in savings.
- Managed a large team of 8 direct reports and over 1,000 indirect reports.
- Through process improvements, made the hospital one of the most profitable in the state.

WORK EXPERIENCE - CONTINUED

Buffalo System Hospital
Buffalo Health, Buffalo, New York   (January 1988 – March 2010)

Buffalo System Hospital is the largest hospital system in upstate New York. Positions held included:

COO/Chief Operating Officer (May 2004 – March 2010)

As the COO for Buffalo Health System, I turned around struggling hospital operations.

- Led the development and implementation of an organizational turnaround strategy and cost reduction for PCU, Rehab and Nutritional Services areas.
- Optimization of process improvements resulted in 250 million dollars in savings in under 4 years.
- Managed a large team of 10 direct reports and over 700 indirect reports.

AVP of Operations (May 2000 – May 2004)

As the AVP of Operations, I turned around the hospital's struggling PCU, Rehab and Nutritional Services areas. Specific duties included:

- Led the development and implementation of an organizational turnaround strategy and cost reduction for PCU, Rehab and Nutritional Services areas.
- Optimization of process improvements resulted in 100 million dollars in savings in under 4 years.

Director of Operations - Surgical Services (November 1998 – May 2000)

As the Director of Operations for Surgical Services, I turned around the hospital's struggling Surgical Services area. Specific duties included:

- Led the development and implementation of an organizational turnaround strategy and cost reduction for Surgical Services.
- Optimization of process improvements resulted in 50 million dollars in savings in under 4 years.

Nurse Manager - Surgical Services (January 1988 – November 1998)

EDUCATION

Formal Education:
MBA – Focus in Healthcare – University of North Carolina
Bachelor of Nursing – University of Buffalo

Professional Certifications:
Registered Nurse – State of New York
Six Sigma Green Belt

RESUME TEMPLATE 5

This is an example of an unemployed accounts payable professional's resume. To give the impression of longer timeframes worked and less time off work, months are left off. As the candidate did not finish his education, his school and program is listed but not his diploma. This still shows some education without saying that it was completed. Also, an in-progress certificate program is added to demonstrate the candidate's initiative to grow his career. Volunteer experience is listed to display more experience. Keywords in the Skills section are added to improve SEO and show skill, even if he was only exposed to that skill. Finally, the job title is woven into the resume to improve SEO.

Peter Smith
111 Hook St • Memphis, Tennessee • 38122

Tel: (111) 111-1111

Email: name@gmail.com

Future-focused **Accounts Payable** professional with a commitment to quality and accuracy seeks a progressive role with a dynamic, growth-oriented organization where exceptional accounts payable and analytical techniques can be leveraged to achieve results.

WORK EXPERIENCE

Match-Stick Limited
HR intern, Denver Colorado

(2014 – 2018)

Match-Stick is one of the leading manufacturers of matchsticks. As an Accounts Payable professional, I accurately processed payments to vendors. Specific duties included:

- Accurately reconciled general ledgers, effectively avoiding costly errors.
- Ensured payments were paid to vendors in a timely manner.
- Monitored bank balances, bank reconciliations, internal audits and prepared financial statements.
- Prepared checks and verified invoice amounts.
- Resolved payment discrepancies, ensuring escalations were handled with great customer experience.

Boomerang Treats
Volunteer Accountant

(2012 – 2013)

Boomerang Treats is a leading dog food manufacturer. As a volunteer in the accounting department, I helped to create Excel spreadsheets to track accounts payable discrepancies.

EDUCATION

Formal Education:
Business Major – Southwest Tennessee Community College

Professional Certifications:
Certified Accounts Payable Professional (CAPP) Certification – In Process

SKILLS

• Microsoft Office (Word, Excel, PowerPoint) • Accounting & Payroll Systems (ADP, JD Edwards, Oracle) • Financial Statements • Accounts Payable/Receivable • Tax Reporting • Bank Reconciliation • General Ledgers • Payroll • Profit & Loss Analysis

CONCLUSION

These five resume examples will hopefully give you a clearer idea of what an effective resume should look like, which in turn can help you land your next role.

5

CREATING AN EFFECTIVE COVER LETTER

Creating an effective cover letter is an essential part of the job-hunting process. If your cover letter is not effective, you might lose out on potential job opportunities. So how do you create an effective cover letter?

HOW TO CREATE AN EFFECTIVE COVER LETTER

The purpose of a cover letter is to sell yourself to recruiters and/or hiring managers and to entice them to look at your resume. There are five main components of a cover letter, and they are:

PART 1: YOUR CONTACT INFO

List your contact info at the top middle of the cover letter, like so:

Fred Smith
111 Hook St • Tampa Florida • 33605
Tel: (111) 111-1111   Email: name@gmail.com

PART 2: THE HIRING MANGER'S CONTACT NAME AND COMPANY INFO

Below is a properly formatted example of this part. Remember to include the date. Whenever possible, refer to the hiring manager by name. It is not necessary to address them as Mr., Mrs., or Ms. If you do not have access to the hiring manager's name, "Attention: Hiring Manager" or a greeting of "Dear Hiring Manager" is acceptable. If you don't have the company's address, look it up on Google. This will show potential employers that you have done your homework. Example:

July 22, 2017

Attention: Michael Jones
Acme Corporation
1234 Acme Acres
Tampa Florida
33605

Dear Michael Jones,

PART 3: INTRODUCTION

This is your introductory statement to potential hiring managers. It should be one paragraph and contain:

- The job you are applying for (including the job number, if there is one)
- Where you saw the job (newspaper, online, a job board, etc.)
- Why you are qualified for the role.

Below is an example.

I am very interested in your position as an **Account Manager**, which was listed on CareerBuilder, **job # 1234**, and would like to submit my application for your approval. With over 5 years of experience hitting sales targets for your competitor, Oink Corporation, I would be an ideal candidate for your position. My key areas of expertise include, but are not limited to, the following:

PART 4: YOUR 5 MAJOR SELLING POINTS

In this section, a continuation of Part 3, put a bulleted list of the top five reasons why you are qualified for the role. This is the most important section for the cover letter; it should shine a spotlight on why you are a good fit. To draw attention to this part, it is a good idea to bold the points. Note the following example.

- **Hit 120% of sales quota by producing over 10 million dollars in revenue.**
- **Top 10 account manager in the company for Revenue Quota in 2017.**
- **Successfully developed new business by landing 12 major accounts.**
- **Executed creative business development techniques to define and develop potential new customers within the specialty wholesale pharmacy market.**
- **Made 2017 Sales Club.**

PART 5: CONCLUSION

Your concluding statement ties the whole cover letter together, emphasizing why you are qualified for the role. Don't forget to say thank you, and repeat your name and contact info. Below is a good sample conclusion.

With all my experience, I would be a great asset to your organization.

Thank you,

Fred Smith
Tel: (111) 111-1111
Email: name@gmail.com

OTHER COVER LETTER TIPS:

- **Do not send a cover letter unless asked to do so.** Cover letters are not always needed when applying for a job. If a job application does not ask for a cover letter, there is no need to send one.
- **Delivery of cover letter.** The most common delivery method is uploading to a company's website. The second most common delivery method for a cover letter is via email. Via email, a hiring manager/recruiter will give you instructions as to which method they would prefer to have your cover letter delivered.
- **Subject line when sending via email.** Don't forget the subject line when sending a cover letter via email. If you are not given a set email delivery format, reference the job you are applying for (including job number) in the subject line. For example: re: Reference to Account Manager Job opening – Job # 1234
- **Keep it brief and to the point.** If you are too wordy,

hiring managers will skip your resume. Use your cover letter to quickly highlight your skills and make the hiring manager want to interview you.

- **Customize your cover letter to the role you are applying for.** It is very important that your cover letter be customized for every job you apply for and be focused on your skills that match the job you are applying for.
- **Bold key words.** To draw attention to key points in your cover letter, bold key words, such as the job you are applying for, the job number (if any), your five bullet points, your name, the hiring managers name and company info.
- **Use proper spelling and grammar.** It goes without saying that your cover letter should be free of errors.

PUTTING IT ALL TOGETHER

The following page shows what a basic cover letter should look like.

Fred Smith

111 Hook St • Tampa Florida • 33605

Tel: (111) 111-1111   Email: name@gmail.com

July 22, 2017

Attention: Michael Jones
Acme Corporation
1234 Acme Acres
Tampa, Florida
33605

Dear Michael Jones,

I am very interested in your position as an **Account Manager**, which was listed on Ca-reerBuilder, **job # 1234**, and would like to submit my application for your approval. With over 5 years of experience hitting sales targets for your competitor, Oink Corporation, I would be an ideal candidate for your position. My key areas of expertise include, but are not limited to, the following:

- **Hit 120% of sales quota by producing over 10 million dollars in revenue.**
- **Top 10 account manager in the company for Revenue Quota in 2017.**
- **Successfully developed new business by landing 12 major accounts.**
- **Executed creative business development techniques to define and develop potential new customers within the specialty wholesale pharmacy market.**
- **Made 2017 Sales Club.**

With all my experience, I would be a great asset to your organization.

Thank you,

Fred Smith
Tel: (111) 111-1111
Email: name@gmail.com

6

CREATING A LINKEDIN PROFILE THAT STANDS OUT

Most job seekers are familiar with LinkedIn (*https://www.linkedin.com/*), one of the world's largest social media sites. For those job seekers who are not, it is a business-centric social media site that allows individuals to create an online profile that works like a resume. Not all LinkedIn users are looking for a job, but users can be contacted by potential employers about job opportunities.

If a recruiter or potential employer is interested in a user's profile, they will contact that person via LinkedIn in-mails or directly via email. If interested, the job seeker can then choose to respond and communicate with the recruiter about potential job offers.

Why is it important to create a LinkedIn profile? You may be able to find jobs on LinkedIn without creating a profile; however, to apply for most jobs on LinkedIn, you submit an application using your LinkedIn profile.

This chapter will teach you how to create an effective LinkedIn profile. A strong profile will increase your chances of being found and contacted by recruiters looking to fill jobs that you might be perfect for.

Please note: LinkedIn's format is constantly changing; therefore, there is a small chance the information in this chapter could change over time.

STEPS TO BUILDING AN EFFECTIVE LINKEDIN PROFILE

Step by step, this section will show you how to build an effective LinkedIn profile that recruiters will find and be interested in. If you already have a LinkedIn profile, use this information to improve your current profile.

STEP 1: REGISTER FOR THE SITE

Registering on LinkedIn is fast and easy. Simply go to *https://www.linkedin.com/* and sign up by entering your first name, last name, and email address. You'll also create a password.

STEP 2 – FIRST INFO REQUESTED BY LINKEDIN

First, you'll be asked to do the following: Choose a country and ZIP/postal code, indicate if you're a a student, and enter your current job title, company, and industry. Below you will find more info on all these areas.

- **Country and ZIP Code/Postal Code.** When creating your LinkedIn profile, make sure you enter the correct country and ZIP code/postal code. (This is like the SEO section in Chapter 5.) When a recruiter searches for LinkedIn profiles, they usually search by location, such as ZIP/postal code and/or city. If you choose the wrong location, you will not appear in the recruiter's search. If you live in a smaller suburb or outlying town, you can choose to list a nearby larger city. Recruiters tend to search in bigger markets, so your best bet is to list your profile in a bigger geographical center.

- **Are you a Student?** This is self-explanatory. If you're a student, click yes. If not, click no.
- **Job Title.** On LinkedIn, like on your resume, use a good job title. Please refer to the Job Titles section in Chapter 4, as that information also applies to LinkedIn job titles.
- **Company.** Type in the full name of your current employer if you have one. If the company you work for is recognizable, it will pop up, and all you need to do is select it. Also, do not use a short form for the company name if people do not know it by that name—doing do will make it harder to find in a search.
- **Industry.** For this section, you will be given a drop-down of different industries to select from. Pick the industry that most closely matches your profession.

STEP 3 – WHAT IS YOUR FOCUS FOR USING THE LINKEDIN PLATFORM?

For this section, you will be asked to choose one of the following options:

- Finding a job
- Staying up to date with my industry
- Building my professional network
- Keeping in touch with my contacts
- Not sure yet. I'm open!

Choose "Finding a job." LinkedIn will then ask you if you want daily or weekly alerts based on your job title and location. My advice to job seekers is to opt for daily alerts.

STEP 4 – UPLOADING YOUR CONTACTS

For this section, LinkedIn will ask if you would like to upload your contacts to see if any of them are already on LinkedIn. I would recommend adding your contacts, as more contacts on LinkedIn gives you more visibility. There is more about this at the end of the chapter.

STEP 5 – CONNECTING WITH PEOPLE LINKEDIN SUGGESTS

In this section, LinkedIn will ask you if you would like to connect with different people. My advice is to select "all especially recruiters." Connecting with as many as possible will put your profile in the eyes of more people. Most people, especially recruiters, will not turn down your request. This is further explained at the end of the chapter.

STEP 6 - UPLOAD A PICTURE

Although you might not be comfortable uploading your picture to LinkedIn, I highly recommend doing so. Recruiters like to see a picture to ascertain that you are indeed a real person; having a picture brings you to life.

There is nothing like a first impression, so make sure your picture looks good. If possible, have your photo professionally taken. In it, you should be wearing the type of clothing you would wear on the job. If you are applying for a white-collar position, wear a suit or other business-appropriate clothing. If you are a nurse, wear scrubs.

STEP 7 – ADD DETAILED INFO INTO YOUR LINKEDIN PROFILE

For this section, you will need to go to your newly-created LinkedIn profile. From there, perfect your profile by adding to the following sections:

- **Background Photo** – This photo is different than your main photo. It is a banner picture (not of you) that goes across your profile header. Choose a background photo that relates to your personality or career. I recommend using one in an overall neutral color, like cream or tan. If you do not have any background pictures, you can get one for free at *https://pixabay.com/*.
- **Headline** – You have one sentence to make a good first impression. The headline is the first thing people

will see in your profile. Treat it like the objective section on your resume. Mention your job title or job interest as well as the key skills you possess. Repeating keywords in various parts of your profile can rank you higher on recruiters' search results and will add to the SEO of your LinkedIn profile. Please note there is a space count for this section, so use your words carefully. A good example headline is:

Leading Contact Center Rep with extensive experience, providing excellent customer service for Fortune 500 companies.

- **Positions** – For this section, add the jobs you have held in chronological order. You can cut and paste this from your resume.
- **Education** – List your education in chronological order. Again, you can cut and paste from your resume.
- **Summary** – This section is like your headline, except you have more space to work with. Use the SEO technique of weaving in keywords and titles to increase the visibility of your profile. You can cut and paste your objective section from your resume; however, you can also add more keywords in your summary section than you can in a typical resume. I would not recommend mentioning that you are looking for a job unless you are currently working. The following is an example of a strong summary. *Results-oriented Senior Java/J2EE Software Developer with a proven track record of delivering software solutions in the financial/banking industry. 7+ years of experience as a Senior Java/J2EE software developer for well-known financial service companies Financial-ecom Inc. & Trading Floor Software Solutions.*
- **Featured Skills & Endorsements** – Add as many

skills as you can. The more you add, the greater the likelihood of your profile popping up when recruiters search for people by keyword(s). The smallest word can be searched by a recruiter, so adding different keywords to this section can increase your chances of being found. For starters, use the keywords from your resume's Skill section. From there, as you did for your resume, research different keywords to add to your profile. The Endorsement section is where people endorse your various skills. The more endorsements you have, the more impressive your profile will appear. To get more endorsements, reach out to your former colleagues and friends and ask them to endorse your skills. Most people will oblige.

- **Volunteer Experience** – As real estate is less of an issue with a LinkedIn profile, I recommend adding volunteer experience to your profile. This section can be especially good for those who do not have much experience or are working or looking to work for an organization that values volunteer work. Be careful not to add things that are too political in nature or that could rub people the wrong way.

STEP 8: ACCOMPLISHMENTS SECTION

This section is an opportunity to add your accomplishments in the following categories: Publications, Certifications, Courses, Projects, Honors & Awards, Patents, Test Scores, Languages, Organizations. If you have any experience or skills in any or all of these categories, I recommend that you add them into your profile. It will increase your chances of being seen by a recruiter.

According to LinkedIn, professionals with publications in their profile are found seven times more than profiles that do not have publications, and profiles that list certifications are found five times more often than profiles that do not list certifications.

OTHER TIPS

BE HONEST AND USE PROPER SPELLING AND GRAMMAR

Like your resume and cover letter, make sure your LinkedIn profile is properly edited for spelling and grammar. And just like your resume, do not lie about your skills, titles, and the companies where you have worked.

GET ENDORSEMENTS ON LINKEDIN

Endorsements give you credibility, so it is recommended you ask many former colleagues to give you positive endorsements. Think of using services based on Yelp reviews or buying products on Amazon based on positive reviews. Your LinkedIn recommendations work like Yelp or Amazon reviews. Aren't you more likely to use a service or buy a product that has good reviews? In the same way, if you include positive endorsements in your LinkedIn profile, potential employers may be more inclined to contact you.

If you have a good relationship with a former colleague and they are on LinkedIn, there is a good chance they will give you a recommendation. To ask for recommendations, go to *https://www.linkedin.com/recs/received*. Click the top middle column,

Ask for Recommendations. A pop-up menu will appear, which asks the following questions:

1. **What do you want to be recommended for?**
   The drop-down menu will list the roles and companies you worked for. Select the role/title you want to be recommended for.
2. **Who do you want to ask?**
   Select who you want to ask for a recommendation from your LinkedIn contacts. It's a good idea to ask your contacts ahead of time if they are willing to give you a recommendation.
3. **What's your relationship?**
   From the drop-down menu, select what your relationship is/was with the person you are asking to recommend you. The second part of this section has a drop-down menu which asks for the person's position at the time. Select the role they had when they worked with you.
4. **Write your message.**
   Using the template provided by LinkedIn, write an InMail asking for their recommendation. Don't forget to include a subject line.

CONNECT WITH PEOPLE TO EXPAND YOUR NETWORK

A great way to grow your network on LinkedIn and increase your chances of being seen by more recruiters is to connect with many people. Here are some tips on how to expand your network:

1. **Upload your contacts into LinkedIn**, see if any are

on the platform, and then connect with them. You can upload Hotmail, Gmail, Yahoo, or Outlook contacts. You can even upload Excel spreadsheets. These contacts will be sent an InMail inviting them to connect. Also, your non-LinkedIn contacts will be given the option to join LinkedIn and connect.

2. **Look up people you have worked with, friends, and family** and invite them to connect. Click the search icon at the top of your main page and type the name you are looking for. You will be shown a list of names along with the option to connect.

3. **Look up recruiters, especially those in your profession**, and send them invites to connect. Most recruiters will accept your invitation. To find recruiters, type "recruiter" in the search box and different recruiter profiles will pop up.

4. **Send invites to people LinkedIn recommends**. To do this, go to *My Network*. Below it, you should see *People You May Know*. A list of people will appear. Under each person's picture is a *Connect* box you can click to add them to your network. Many people will accept your invite request. Be careful on this one—LinkedIn will warn you if you try to connect to too many people who've rejected your request.

5. **Connect with people in your field**, especially hiring managers. To look them up, hit the search icon and type 'hiring manager'. You'll be taken to a page where you can search for hiring managers by company and title. By connecting with people in your industry, especially hiring managers, more eyes will be on your profile.

6. **Look for open networkers**. These are people on LinkedIn who are open to connecting with anyone. In the search

bar, type "Lion" or "Open Networker" to find profiles.

7. **Always except connections** when invited to connect on LinkedIn. It will expand your network. Remember, LinkedIn is not like Facebook; the purpose of LinkedIn is to make business connections.

JOIN LINKEDIN GROUPS

Joining professional groups can expand your reach. Recruiters look at these groups to find talent and post jobs. To use this feature, go to the search bar. Click the *Work* icon, found at the top right corner, and look for the *Groups* icon. Hit the *Groups* icon and a page will come up that gives you recommendations (based on your job title) of groups to join.

CONCLUSION

By creating a detailed and SEO-centric LinkedIn page, connecting with contacts, and joining groups, your profile will attract attention. You will easily be found by recruiters. That translates into more job opportunities for you.

7

HOW TO LOOK FOR A JOB ON LINKEDIN

The last chapter focused on how to create an effective LinkedIn profile. This chapter will focus on how to look for jobs on LinkedIn. It will teach you four different ways to find jobs on this platform.

Please note: LinkedIn is constantly changing their format. Therefore, there is a small chance the information in this chapter could change over time.

LINKEDIN JOB ALERTS

The easiest and fastest way to search for a job on LinkedIn is to create job alerts. The steps are outlined below:

Step 1 – Log into your LinkedIn account and find the *Jobs* icon (in the top middle). Click this icon. It will bring you to the Jobs page.

Step 2 – On the Jobs page, hit the *Search* icon in the right upper corner. This will bring you to the Search page.

Step 3 – In the left corner, you will see options to set for your job alerts. They include Location, Company, Date Posted, Experience Level, Industry, and Job Function.

- **Location** – For this section, I recommend choosing the main city near your home.
- **Company** – I recommend keeping this section blank, as listing companies might limit your search.
- **Date Posted** – Click "Any time" to expand your search to all jobs listed.
- **Experience Level** – Select the option that reflects your current experience level. For example, if you are a new grad, click "Entry Level". You can also select more than one level.
- **Industry** – If you work in a specific industry, like healthcare, select that industry. If you do not work in a specific industry, keep it open. If you do not see your industry, hit *Add* and enter your profession. If you do not see your profession, keep it blank. You can also select more than one industry.
- **Job Function** – For this section, select your job function. For example, if you work in accounting, select accounting. If you do not see your job function, hit *Add* and enter your job function. Try to find the closest match to your skill set. You can also select more than one job function.

Step 4 – Hit *Create Job Alert* and all your selections will populate. Choose how often you want LinkedIn to send you emails about jobs. I recommend daily alerts so you do not miss opportunities. You also have the option of getting both email and mobile alerts. I would recommend both. After hitting *Save*, you should start receiving job alerts.

HOW TO SEARCH FOR JOB POSTINGS

Job alerts are a great way to find jobs on LinkedIn, but you could miss out on some jobs because they will not show up on alerts. Therefore, check LinkedIn daily for jobs postings. Here's how to find and apply for jobs:

Step 1 – Log into your LinkedIn account and in the top middle, you will find the *Jobs* icon. Click on it. This will bring you to the Jobs page.

Step 2 – On the Jobs page, in the top right corner, you will find two search bars. In the first search bar, you can search for jobs by typing in job titles, keywords, and companies. In the second search bar (to the right of the first search bar), you can search for jobs by location (city, state, postal code) or country.

Step 3 – After typing in your keywords, jobs will populate. In most cases, you can apply for them with one click using Easy Apply. When you choose Easy Apply, you apply using your LinkedIn profile. In some cases, when you click on the job, you will either be taken to the employer's website or be asked to fill out an application.

HOW TO FIND JOBS ON LINKEDIN GROUPS

Many job seekers ignore LinkedIn groups; this could lead them to miss out on jobs, as some recruiters post jobs directly to groups. The previous chapter discussed how to join groups, so please refer to that section. To find jobs in LinkedIn groups, follow these steps:

Step 1 – Log into your LinkedIn account. In the upper right corner, you will find the *Work* icon. Click that icon; you will find the *Groups* icon in the drop-down menu. Click *Groups* and it will bring you to your Groups page.

Step 2 – On the top of the Groups page, click *My Groups*. This will pull up all the groups you belong to.

Step 3 – Hit one of your groups and it will take you to that group's page.

Step 4 – In that group's page, a third of the way down, you will find the word Job in small writing. It is found just below the *Start a Conversation with Your Group* section. (It is in a small font, so look for it carefully.) Hit the *Job* icon and it will take you to a page that lists job postings by recruiters.

Step 5 – Look through the jobs and click the jobs you are interested in. Once you select a job, the recruiter will provide instruction on how to apply, such as sending a resume or applying online. Also, some groups have job alerts that you can receive via email.

LOOKING FOR JOBS IN YOUR FEED SECTION

The final way to look for jobs on LinkedIn is to use your feed. Many recruiters post jobs on their LinkedIn feed, which lets them advertise their jobs for free. This is probably the least effective way to look for jobs on LinkedIn, as it can be very time-consuming and hit-and-miss in terms of effectiveness. There is value in looking for jobs on your feed, but don't spend your whole day at it.

To look for jobs on your feed, simply scroll down on your LinkedIn main page and look for postings about jobs. Usually, the recruiter will include a link to apply or they will provide contact info to learn more about the role.

CONCLUSION

LinkedIn provides four distinct ways to look for and find jobs: receiving job alerts, through LinkedIn job posting sections, in groups, and on your LinkedIn feed. By taking advantage of all four of these job search avenues, you will find more jobs to apply for.

8

THE IMPORTANCE OF SPEED

One of the most common places you will search for a job is on a job board. A job board is a website where employers post roles that need to be filled. Job boards can vary in size from large boards (like CareerBuilder) to niche boards (like Dice, an IT job board). There are also hundreds of smaller boards, including regional boards and boards in almost every job sector.

Related to job boards are aggregators, or indexed job sites such as Indeed and Glassdoor. Aggregators take jobs from many sources and put them together in one place.

In the following chapters, you will be given more information on the major job boards and aggregators, as well as links to many niche and smaller job boards.

THE IMPORTANCE OF SPEED

An overlooked part of applying for jobs is speed.

Every day you delay applying for a job, another person applies for that same job. Before you know it, the employer has enough candidates and closes the job. You have missed out.

Employers do not wait for latecomers to submit applications. Usually, the first people to apply have the greatest chance of getting roles. It is common practice for employers to close roles when they have enough candidates in their pipeline.

To ensure you're on the top of the list, apply to roles as soon as you see them open. Delaying by even a few hours is bad enough, but waiting days could cost you that potential job opportunity.

How do you find jobs before others do? Sign up for job alerts. Make sure that you check for new job postings every day.

JOB ALERTS

One of the biggest ways a job seeker can save time is to create job alerts. Job alerts are daily or weekly emails that are sent to job seekers to inform them about open jobs. The seeker simply signs up for alerts based on the jobs they are interested in. All the major job boards and aggregators have a job alert option; they will be covered in the following chapters.

QUICK APPLY APPLICATIONS

Another great way to save time in your job search is to use Quick Apply applications. This great tool gives job seekers the option of applying for jobs in a few clicks. On most major sites, you are given the option to Quick Apply for some jobs. What these sites cleverly have done is allow you to apply to jobs with the resume or profile you've already uploaded to the site. In the case of Indeed and LinkedIn, the job list tells you what jobs offer the Quick Apply process. You can save tons of time by applying to many jobs with one easy Quick Apply process.

CONCLUSION

Job boards are one of the most common ways to apply for a job, but they are just the start. By using extra features - such as job alerts and Quick Apply applications - you will be able to apply for more jobs in less time.

9

LOOKING FOR JOBS ON INDEED

Indeed (*http://www.indeed.com/*) is the largest job site, with over 250 million unique visitors each month, and it's growing.

Indeed, unlike traditional job boards, works more like a search engine, so it falls under the job aggregator category. Job aggregators are essentially job board search engines that collect job postings across the internet and make them easily searchable under one page. Indeed lists paid sponsored jobs at the top of the search results, followed by jobs based on relevant keywords.

This chapter will explain how to create a resume profile and apply for jobs on Indeed. Because Indeed is the world's largest job site, it is important you learn this chapter well.

Please note: Indeed is always changing, so some steps may change over time.

HOW TO CREATE A RESUME PROFILE ON INDEED

The great thing about Indeed is that it's user friendly and very easy to create a profile.

Why is it so important to create a resume profile? Indeed is the most popular tool used by recruiters to find candidates for job roles. Creating a profile also gives you the ability to apply for jobs directly on Indeed. Many jobs allow you to Quick Apply using your Indeed resume.

Let's go through each step of the process of creating an effective resume profile on Indeed:

Step 1 – Go to *https://www.indeed.com/*. On the main page, find the *Upload Your Resume* button below the two search bars at the top. Click it.

Step 2 – On this page, you have the choice of uploading your resume or building one. I recommend uploading your resume. It will be faster and easier.

Step 3 – Upload your resume. Click *Next*, which will prompt you to input your email and confirm your email address.

Step 4 – Go to your email and confirm your email address. You will be sent back to Indeed to complete your application.

Step 5 – Create a password. After you've completed the signup, you'll be sent to your resume page to complete your resume.

Step 6 – Once you are back on your resume page, carefully look to ensure that your resume was properly uploaded into your Indeed profile and no important information is missing. If anything is missing, add it now. Make sure that you completely fill out the main sections: Profile, Desired Job, Work Experience, and Education.

Step 7 – Indeed has sections that most resumes do not have, including Skills, Military Service, Awards, Certifications/ Licenses, Groups, Patents, Publications, and Additional Information. You should fill in as much of these sections as you can. The more info you include, the greater your chance of being seen on recruiters' searches. Below you will find more information on each section:

- **Skills** – The more skills you have, the better. Recruiters often search by keywords when looking to fill roles; adding different keywords to your skills can increase your chances of being found (even the smallest keywords count).

- **Links** – This is where you can add links to your LinkedIn profile, website, or other online portfolios.

- **Military Service** – In certain countries, like the US, there are employers who value military service. In some countries, veterans are put in the special interest groups category, which means companies are given a certain quota of hires out of that group. This being the case, you should list your military service if you live a country that values it.

- **Awards** – List any relevant awards you have won, including scholarships, company awards, achievements, or any other work-related accomplishment.

- **Certifications/Licenses** – List all relevant certifications and licenses you have, including those that are in progress or that you plan to do.

- **Groups** – List all organizations you belong to in your industry and any volunteer organizations.

- **Patents** – List patents you've been awarded, if you have any.

- **Publications** – If you have written for any publications or published any articles or books, include that information here.

- **Additional Information** – Any other relevant information not covered above. For example, you could add the Objective section of your resume to boost your SEO.

Step 8 – Finally, make sure your resume is **viewable** by checking the *Public* box. By making your resume public, more people can find your profile.

CREATING JOB ALERTS ON INDEED

Like most job boards, Indeed allows you to create job alerts to daily notify you about job opportunities. Indeed bases its job alerts on searches you have done. For instance, if you search for "Teacher in Hartford," you will be sent similar jobs in your alert. You can set up job alerts in two easy steps.

Step 1 – Click your email icon in the top right corner. In the drop-down menu, choose *My Subscriptions*.

Step 2 – On the Subscriptions page, it asks if you would like to receive daily emails. Select *Get a Daily Email with Recommended Jobs*. You will also be given the option of receiving other marketing emails. I would not check the marketing email box because you will receive emails about non-relevant jobs and other solicitations.

QUICK APPLY JOBS ON INDEED

The great thing about Indeed is the ability to Quick Apply for jobs. Some jobs allow you to apply by simply clicking the job and then hitting the *Apply* button. Quick Apply uses your Indeed resume profile instead of having to go through a long application process, which saves a ton of time. It also allows you to apply for many jobs in a short amount of time.

LOOKING FOR JOBS ON INDEED

Because Indeed lists more jobs than any other job site, it is crucial that you look on Indeed each day. You also need to correctly use the Search tool. Indeed offers both basic and advanced searches; using these effectively will help you find the jobs you're looking for.

BASIC JOB SEARCHES

Indeed makes basic searches super easy. Go to the *Find Jobs* section. There you will find two search bars. One is *What*, which is the job title you are looking for. The other is *Where*, which is the location where you want to work. Enter the job you are looking for in *What* and the job location in *Where* and click the *Find Jobs* button. Different jobs will pop up. Apply for the ones that meet your criteria.

ADVANCED JOB SEARCHES

The difference between basic and advanced job search is that the advanced search allows you to look up jobs using more defined criteria. I recommend this option for many cases, as you can be very exact and avoid looking at jobs that do not match your needs. Below, we'll explain each step in using the advanced job search function.

Step 1 – On the Find Jobs page, click *Advanced Job Search*, found in right middle corner beneath the *Find Jobs* button.

Step 2 - On the Advanced Job Search page, you will find the following categories: *With All of These Words, With the Exact Phrase, With At Least One of These Words, With None of These Words, With These Words in the Title, From This Company, Show Jobs of Type, Show Jobs From, Salary Estimate, Location, Age, Display,* and *Relevance/Date.* Let's go through each of these options:

- **With All of These Words** – This category is for searching keywords. For example, if you were looking for a C# developer job, you might enter the keyword "C#."
- **With the Exact Phrase** – Use this category when you want to find a specific job title or type of job. For example, enter the exact phrase "entry level" if you are looking for an entry level job.
- **With At Least One of These Words** –Use this category if you're looking for a certain type of job. In this case, the keywords don't have to be in any particular order. For example, if you were looking for jobs only in the pharmaceutical industry, choose this option and enter "pharmaceutical" into the search box.
- **With None of These Words** – This category helps you narrow down your search by eliminating jobs that contain an unwanted word. For example, if you are looking for a customer service job but do not want one that requires a

quota, you would type "quota" and no jobs with the word quota in the description will pop up.

- **With These Words in the Title** – Using this option, you can look for jobs with keywords in the title. For example, if you were looking for an accountant job in accounts payable you might type "accounts payable" to ensure those jobs pop up in the search results.

- **From This Company** – In this search option, you can search for jobs being posted by a specific company. For example, if you wanted to work for the Acme Corporation, you would type that in the search. For the most part, I would not recommend using this category because it will greatly limit your search.

- **Show Jobs of Type** – This is a drop-down menu which gives you the option of choosing the type of job you are interested in: All Job Types, Full-time, Part-time, Contract, Internship, Temporary.

- **Show Jobs From** – This is a drop-down menu which gives you the choice of what sites you want to use: *All Web Sites, Job Boards Only*, or *Employer Web Sites Only*. For the most part, I would keep it open (by selecting *All Web Sites*) because you will have access to more jobs.

- **Salary Estimate** – In this section, select a yearly salary range, such as $50,000 or $40K-$90K. For the most part, I would not recommend putting anything in this section because many companies do not include salary in their job listings.

- **Location** – Select the location of the job you are searching for, either by city or by ZIP/postal code. From a drop-down menu, select how long of a commute (from your specified location) you want: *Only In* (location), *Within 5 Miles of, Within 10 Miles of, Within 15 Miles of, Within*

25 Miles of, or *Within 50 Miles of*. For example, if you are looking for a job within a 15-mile radius of Milwaukee, Wisconsin, you would select *Within 15 Miles* of and enter "Milwaukee, WI" in the location box. If you wanted a more exact search, type in a ZIP/postal code and select *Within 15 Miles of* in the drop-down.

- **Age** – For this section, select from the drop-down menu how old a job you want to search for. In other words, you're choosing how long that job has been posted. The drop-down choices are: *Anytime, Within 15 Days, Within 7 Days, Within 3 Days, Since Yesterday,* and *Since My Last Visit*. When you first start using the tool, I recommend choosing *Anytime*. When you have done a few advanced searches and have seen many of the old jobs, change to *Yesterday* or *Since My Last Visit* to only be shown new jobs.

- **Display** and **Relevance/Date** – These sections allow you to choose how many jobs you want to see per page and how you'd like them displayed (by relevance or by the date the job was posted). Relevance will show you jobs that are the most relevant to your search criteria, so that's what I recommend.

CONCLUSION

By following the advice given in this chapter, a job seeker will be able to create effective Indeed profiles and apply for jobs on the world's largest job platform.

10

LOOKING FOR JOBS ON ZIPRECRUITER

ZipRecruiter (*https://www.ziprecruiter.com/*) is one of the fastest-growing job sites. It works differently than most job boards, posting jobs from hundreds of job boards and websites. Another great advantage of using ZipRecruiter is getting email job alerts. I highly recommend using this tool to search for jobs and to be easily found by employers.

Please note: As with all the other job boards, ZipRecruiter is always changing their format, so over time some of this information may change.

HOW TO CREATE A RESUME PROFILE ON ZIPRECRUITER

Creating a resume profile on ZipRecruiter makes it easy for recruiters to find you by searching the ZipRecruiter database. It also allows you to get job alerts from employers.

Here's how to create a resume profile on ZipRecruiter.

Step 1 – Go to *https://www.ziprecruiter.com/contact/create* and you will be taken to a page to register for an account. To register, you will need to fill in three sections: *Enter Your Basic Info, Create a Job Alert*, and *Upload Your Resume*. Below you will find more information on all three.

- **Enter Your Basic Info** – Enter your name and email address.
- **Create a Job Alert** – This section allows you to get daily email job alerts. Type in the title of the job you're looking for and your desired location(either by city and state or ZIP code). Most job alerts will let you apply for jobs with one click. Signing up for daily email alerts is not required, but I highly recommend it.
- **Upload Your Resume** – Upload your existing resume and then click the *Create Account* button at the bottom.

Step 2 – After you complete the registration, ZipRecruiter will give you the option of signing up for job alerts by text. I recommend doing this; you'll have the advantage of getting real-time job alerts sent right to your phone. You'll be able to apply for jobs before other job seekers who do not use this feature.

HOW TO LOOK FOR JOBS ON ZIPRECRUITER

Looking for jobs on ZipRecruiter is a simple process. It might very well be the easiest job site to use.

There are four ways to look for jobs on ZipRecruiter:

1. Sign up for email job alerts, which you should have already done when you registered.

2. Sign up for mobile job alerts.
3. Look for jobs under Suggested Jobs, which is found in the top right corner when you are logged into the system. It will bring up jobs based on your job title.
4. Search for jobs by job title and location. It is just like setting up job alerts.

You can Quick Apply to many of the jobs you find on ZipRecruiter. For jobs that don't support Quick Apply, you'll be redirected to the employer's website or landing page to apply for the job.

CONCLUSION

Creating a resume and looking for jobs on ZipRecruiter is essential because it is one of the fastest-growing job sites.

11

LOOKING FOR JOBS ON GLASSDOOR

Glassdoor (*https://www.glassdoor.com*) is the top employee-review website. Current or past employees give reviews about their experiences working for a particular organization. A company is given a rating from 1 to 5, with 5 being high and 1 being low. Along with the reviews, employees can leave comments about their experiences with an employer. Not only is Glassdoor a company review site, it is also a job aggregator; it lists many job openings employers have posted, including sponsored jobs.

Because Glassdoor is one of the fastest-growing job aggregators, it is important to look for jobs on this site. In this chapter, you will learn how to look for jobs on Glassdoor.

Please note: Glassdoor is always changing their format, so some steps may change over time.

HOW TO CREATE A PROFILE ON GLASSDOOR

Step 1 – Go to *https://www.glassdoor.com*. Click the *Sign In* button found at the top. A box will pop up and below the box you will see "Don't have an account? Sign Up". Click *Sign Up*.

Step 2 – At the signup page, enter your email and create a password. Then click *Create Your Account*.

Step 3 – On this new page, enter your job title and location and hit *Continue*. A new box will pop up that prompts you to fill in more info, including employer name and company, and to upload your resume. After you do all this, click *Continue*.

Step 4 – The next page will ask you to rate a company. You can skip this by hitting *Skip for Now*.

Step 5 – The next page will ask for more information, such as Salary Details, Job Details, Gender, and whether you're a current or former employee. I recommend skipping these things, as some of it is too personal. You can do this by hitting *Skip*.

Step 6 – Go to your email and verify your account by hitting *Activating Account*. This will allow you to set up job alerts and apply to jobs using Quick Apply (where available).

HOW TO LOOK FOR JOBS ON GLASSDOOR

Step 1 – Go to *https://www.glassdoor.com* and click *Jobs* in the top left corner.

Step 2 – On the Jobs page, you can search for jobs in three different ways:
- **Title, Keywords or Company** – Search for jobs either by

job title, keywords, or company.

- **Location** – Search for jobs by location (i.e. by typing the name of the city where you are looking for a job).
- **Jobs** – In the drop-down menu, you are given a choice of searching by jobs, companies, salaries, or interviews. Choose jobs, as that is what you want to search for.

Step 3 – After hitting the green *Submit* button at the top right, you will be taken to a new page where the results generated by your search will appear. Apply to the jobs you are interested in. On this page, you'll also be given the option to set up job alerts. Click the *Job Alerts* icon to be notified about jobs similar to those you just searched for.

HOW TO FIND EMPLOYER REVIEWS

Make use of the employer reviews Glassdoor provides. Reviews will help you determine if a potential employer would be a good fit for you or not. Here's how to look up employer reviews:

Step 1 – Go to *https://www.glassdoor.com/Reviews/index.htm.*

Step 2 – On this page, you can search reviews by company and location. In the search bar, type in the company you're investigating, then click *Search*. On the next page, the results of your search will appear. You can look at the company's overall rating as well as more in-depth information about the company, such as overview, reviews, jobs, salaries, interviews, and benefits.

CONCLUSION

More and more job openings are being posted on Glassdoor. Therefore, it is advantageous to make use of this tool in your job search. In addition, Glassdoor is a great source for checking company reviews and other valuable information, such as salaries and benefits.

12

LOOKING FOR JOBS ON FACEBOOK

Facebook (*https://www.facebook.com/*) is the largest social media site; as of 2019, it has about 2.4 billion active users.

Most job seekers already have a Facebook profile, but they do not realize that they can search for jobs on Facebook. Having a detailed Facebook profile also increases the likelihood of recruiters finding you and sending you ads about jobs.

This chapter will show you how to look for jobs on Facebook. You'll also learn what information to add to your profile so that you will pop up on recruiters' radar.

SEARCHING FOR JOB ADS ON FACEBOOK

Facebook has a new feature that allows some users to look for jobs. It is a relatively new feature, so the search might be limited. Still, it's worth seeing what job ads are out there. Here's how to look for a job on Facebook.

Step 1 – Go to *https://www.facebook.com/jobs*.

Step 2 – On the Jobs page, you can search for jobs based on the city you have listed on your Facebook profile. You can search for jobs by industry or job type or by entering keywords into the search bar in the top left corner. If you find a job you like in the search results, select *Apply Now* and you will be taken to the company's landing page to apply for the job.

LOOKING FOR JOBS IN FACEBOOK GROUPS

Another place to look for jobs on Facebook is in Facebook groups. Many professions have set up groups on Facebook where, in some cases, jobs are posted by recruiters, hiring managers, or even helpful members of the same profession. You can find groups and use them in your job in two easy steps:

Step 1 – Log into your Facebook account and type your profession in the top search bar. For example, if you are a nurse, you would type "nurse." Different nurse-themed Facebook pages will be shown, and scrolling down, you will find Groups for Nurses. The best group to join might be one geared towards jobs, such as Nurse Jobs. Most professions have groups like this. Click *Join* to join the group.

Step 2 – After you get a notification that you are approved, you can look to see if the group has threads about jobs. If it does, look for the ones that interest you and apply. Not all groups have posts about jobs. If they do not, you can leave the group.

POST THAT YOU ARE LOOKING FOR A JOB

In your group, unless it restricts posts, you can try posting that you are looking for a job. Recruiters, hiring managers, and members of your profession might see your post and send you job ads. Or they might refer you to people they know who have job openings.

Make sure that your post is simple and to the point, for example: "Looking for a new role as an RN in Philadelphia. If someone knows of any roles, please let me know."

HOW TO GET MORE ADS ABOUT JOBS ON YOUR FACEBOOK FEED

Have you ever gotten ads on your Facebook feed? Many people get targeted ads based on their Facebook profile.

Job ads are no different. Some recruiters will set up ads targeted to a certain audience. By selecting specific job titles and companies, their ad will be sent to Facebook profiles that match those keywords. For example, if a recruiter was looking to reach Java Developers in San Jose, they would set up a Facebook ad with the keywords "San Jose", "Java" and "developer." Facebook users who live near San Jose and have the words "Java" and "developer" in their profiles would get that ad on their feed.

How do you add keywords to your Facebook profile so that you will be selected to receive job ads?

Step 1 – Go to your Facebook page and click on the About icon at the top.

Step 2 – In the About page, fill in more information

about yourself, specifically: education, job titles, and companies where you have worked.

HELP RECRUITERS FIND YOUR FACEBOOK PAGE

Help recruiters find your Facebook profile by listing all the job titles you've held and all the companies you've worked for. Recruiters often search for job candidates by using companies and job titles as keywords, so having these in your Facebook profile increases the chances of them finding you. They might contact you about jobs by emailing you on Facebook or finding your contact information.

CONCLUSION

Facebook is more than just a fun social media site; it can also be a great tool to look for jobs. Remember to increase your visibility by including your job history and education in your profile. Recruiters and employers just might send you ads about job opportunities.

13

LOOKING FOR JOBS ON GOOGLE

If you were to survey most job seekers, one of the first places they'd start their job search is Google (*https://www.google.com/*).

WHAT IS A SEARCH ENGINE?

A search engine is a website that sorts websites by how relevant they are to a person's search.

There are many search engines, such as Google, Yahoo, Bing, DuckDuckGo, and more. Any of these search engines can be used to find jobs. Currently, Google is the best job-search option, so this chapter will focus on Google.

POSITIVES AND NEGATIVES OF LOOKING FOR JOBS USING SEARCH ENGINES

The positive: Search engines may find jobs that do not appear on job boards and other job search tools.

The negative: Sometimes a search engine will bring up

irrelevant information or unrelated paid ads that could cost you valuable time. To help ensure you get relevant results, use Boolean techniques to improve the quality of your search. The following section explains how to use this technique.

USING A BOOLEAN SEARCH

If you are not familiar with Boolean, it involves using sequences of command words to help search engines find information. Boolean searches can help you find relevant information and find it faster. Below, you will learn how to use basic Boolean commands, which can be used to search for jobs on Google and other search engines.

BASIC BOOLEAN COMMANDS

The first step in mastering Boolean is to understand basic Boolean commands. There are eight main basic Boolean operators: *AND, OR, NOT, near,* brackets, quotations, *site,* and *inurl.*

1. **AND** - This command links two things together when doing a search. For example: *C++ AND capital markets.* This would prompt a search of C++ and capital markets together. This is a good way to add things to a search.

2. **OR** – This command can link words together when doing a search. For example: *RN OR Registered Nurse.* This would prompt a search for either RN or Registered Nurse. This is a good time-saver because some things can be searched two ways and OR helps

you do that at the same time.

3. **NOT** – This command means you want to exclude a specific word when doing a search. For example, you may want to search for the word "engineer" while excluding anything to do with electrical engineering. For this search, you would type *engineer NOT electrical*. This is a good way to filter unwanted results from a search.

4. **Near** – This command means you want words to appear near each other. For example: *ICU near nurse*. If the words 'ICU' and 'nurse' are found close together on a website, this command will find them in a search. This search is great at finding things that go together that might not appear side by side.

5. **Brackets ( )** – This command will focus the search on whatever word is placed in brackets. For example: *(J2EE)*. By putting 'J2EE' in brackets, the focus of the search will be on J2EE.

6. **Quotations " "** – This command finds exact, word-for-word phrases. For example, if you want to find only Pharmaceutical Sales Representative jobs, you would type *"Pharmaceutical Sales Representative"* in the Google search box.

7. **site:** - Limits your search to one domain. For example: *site:LinkedIn*.

8. **inurl:** - Limits your search to words found in a URL. For example, if you wanted to find resume websites, you would type *inurl:resume*.

GOOGLE'S AGGREGATION OF OTHER JOB SITES

In 2107, Google started aggregating jobs with their partnered job sites. Basically, Google, with their partnered job sites, lists jobs when you type in keywords. For example, if you type "sales job Kentucky" into the Google search box, one of the first things you'll see will be sales jobs in Kentucky from Google's partnered job sites.

WAYS TO SEARCH FOR JOBS ON GOOGLE

To help you make better use of Google to find jobs, I've included three sample searches for different professions. Each example has a simple search and a more complex Boolean search. The simple search will be easier to use, but the Boolean will give you more relevant information.

You can use these examples as a template for your own search; just enter your own keywords, titles, and locations.

First Example: Looking for a Teaching job in Anchorage, Alaska
- **Simple search** – Type in the Google search bar: *teaching jobs in Anchorage.*
- **Complex search** – Type in the Google search bar: *Teacher or Teaching (job or jobs or career or opening or openings) near Anchorage Alaska.*

Second Example: Looking for a Java or J2EE Developer job in Toronto, Canada
- **Simple search** – Type in the Google search bar: *Java*

Developer job in Toronto Canada.
- **Complex search** – Type in the Google search bar: *(job or jobs or career or opening or openings) ("software developer" OR "software engineer" OR programmer OR "software design engineer") (near Toronto) (Java OR j2EE)*

Third Example: Looking for a CFO job in a hospital but not at a home health or Rehabilitation center.
- **Simple search** – Type in the Google search bar: *CFO jobs hospital.*
- **Complex search** – Type in the Google search bar: *CFO or "Chief Financial Officer" AND (job or jobs or career or opening or openings) AND (Hospital or Health System) NOT ("Home Health" and Rehabilitation").*

CONCLUSION

Google is the largest search engine and many jobs can be found by using this tool, so it's a good idea to use Google regularly to search for jobs. In addition, if you learn how to use Boolean searches effectively, you might find jobs other job seekers will not, meaning you'll have less competition.

14

LOOKING FOR JOBS ON CAREERBUILDER

CareerBuilder (*http://www.careerbuilder.com/*), one of the longest-running job boards, has a loyal following among recruiters. Using CareerBuilder to reach this audience can be advantageous. This chapter will teach you how to take full advantage of CareerBuilder, build a resume, and find a job.

Please note: CareerBuilder is always changing their format, so some of the information in this chapter may have changed.

HOW TO BUILD A RESUME ON CAREERBUILDER

Putting a resume on CareerBuilder will allow you to be seen by recruiters who have paid access to the CareerBuilder database. Some jobs on CareerBuilder offer one-click Quick Apply, which will save you time by allowing you to rapidly apply for many jobs.

You can build a resume on CareerBuilder in five simple steps.

Step 1 - Go to *http://www.careerbuilder.com/* and click the *Add Your Resume* button at the top center.

Step 2 – You'll be taken to a signup page. At the bottom of the page, look for the phrase, "Don't have an account? Create One." Hit *Create One.*

Step 3 – This page asks you for the following information to set up your account: first name, last name, email, ZIP code, and password (which you'll need to confirm). Fill in this info and check the boxes labeled "Job Recommendations based on your activity" and "Resume and Application Activity Alerts when your application is viewed." The first option will send you job alerts and the second one will notify you when your application is viewed. Finally, hit the *Sign Up* button at the bottom of the screen.

Step 4 – You will be taken to a new page to fill in more information, such as your desired job title, and to upload a resume. As in other job boards, use your existing resume. Finally, it will ask you about privacy settings. To enable recruiters to see you and contact you, select *Display My Resume and Contact Info.* Click the *Continue* button at the bottom.

Step 5 – On this next page, you will be able to look at your Career Builder profile and make sure that everything transferred over from your resume. If something is missing, you can edit or add the info. At the top of your profile, it shows how many people have viewed your resume. This is a handy tool. In addition, you have the option to add additional sections to your profile, such as Salary, Skills & Qualifications, Relocation Locations, and Contact Information. Below are my recommendations for these sections:

- **Salary** – Keep this section blank so as not to lose out on job opportunities.

- **Skills & Qualifications** – List as many different skills as you can. This makes it easier for recruiters to find you when they do keyword searches based on skills and qualifications.
- **Relocation Locations** – List any city you would be interested in moving to. You can add more than one city by clicking *Add Relocation Information*.

HOW TO SEARCH FOR JOBS ON CAREERBUILDER

Searching for jobs on CareerBuilder is a simple two-step process, explained below.

Step 1 - Go to *http://www.careerbuilder.com/* and click the green *Find Jobs* button in the top corner.

Step 2 – CareerBuilder gives you two search options when searching for roles. In the first search bar, you can search for jobs based on job title, skills, or company. In the second search bar, you can search for jobs based on city, state or ZIP code. In the right corner, you are given more options to refine your search, including Date Posted, Employment Type, Annual Pay, Company, Job Category, and CareerBuilder Apply Only. Below is some information on each option:

- **Date Posted** – Select how old of a job you want to include in your search. The options are 24 hours, 3 days, 7 days, and 30 days. When you first start looking for jobs, keep it open to 30 days. After you have done a few searches, change your selection to 24 hours to find only recently posted jobs.

- **Employment Type** – Select what type of job type you want: All, Full Time, Part Time, Contractor, Contract to Hire, Intern, or Seasonal/Temp. You can select more than one option.
- **Annual Pay** – Keep this section open so as not to limit your search.
- **Company** – You can search for roles by company. I would recommend not doing this unless you are targeting specific companies.
- **Job Category** - You can select up to three job categories.
- **CareerBuilder Apply Only** – Select 'No' so as not to limit your search to jobs that only use the CareerBuilder Apply feature.

CONCLUSION

Creating a resume and looking for jobs on CareerBuilder will allow you to be seen by more recruiters and have access to more job opportunities.

15

DEVELOPING ELATIONSHIPS WITH RECRUITERS

In most jobs you apply for, there is a good chance that at some point you will interact with a recruiter. Because they play such a big role in most job searches, it is important to learn how to develop relationships with both corporate and agency recruiters. This chapter will teach you how to develop relationships with recruiters, which can help you increase your chances of finding a job faster.

WHY AGENCY RECRUITERS ARE IMPORTANT TO YOUR JOB SEARCH

Many job seekers talk about the mystical hidden job market as if it is some far-off land like Atlantis. The truth is, there is a hidden job market that many job seekers ignore: agency recruiters.

Many companies use recruitment agencies if they cannot fill jobs internally. Companies will also use agencies if they do not have the capacity to fill roles or do not have their own internal recruitment department.

For some roles, recruiters have the exclusive domain of recruiting for these jobs. If you are not connected to that recruiter's job, you will not be able to apply to it. With many jobs in the market under agency recruiters' control, it is paramount you make connections with them. Only then will be you able to apply for those jobs. The latter parts of this chapter will go into detail about how to achieve this.

One final point about working with agency recruiters: You do not pay a cent to them if you get hired. Agency recruitment firms are paid by the company that hires you; on average, this fee is about 20% of your first year's salary. In the case of a contract job, they get paid an hourly rate on top of your hourly rate. Avoid any recruitment agency that tries to charge you a fee; they are most likely scamming you. In addition, there is no such thing as one recruiter having exclusive 'rights' to a job seeker. In fact, it is recommended that you connect with multiple recruiters. Having multiple recruiters working for you will increase your odds of finding a job, since each recruiter could have a separate set of clients.

WHY ARE THERE SO MANY INCOMPETENT RECRUITERS?

Over years of interacting with job seekers, I've repeatedly been told that many of the recruiters they have been in contact with have been incompetent.

Unfortunately, in some cases this stereotype can be true. There is an easy entrance path to the recruitment industry, with no certification needed and no governing regulatory body.

Therefore, many recruiters are not properly trained. When these untrained recruiters interact with job seekers, they are not able to fully help them. (Incompetency in the recruitment field is so widespread that I was prompted to write a bestselling book addressing this issue, *Recruiting 101: The Fundamentals of Being a Great Recruiter*.)

This is not to paint a bleak picture. There are some very good recruiters out there. But if you do run across an incompetent recruiter, you must learn to work with them. This chapter will teach you how to do that. You'll learn how to think like a recruiter, which will help you build a resume with recruiters in mind. I'll teach you how to make an impression with recruiters. And finally, you'll learn how to connect with recruiters with the goal of developing long-term relationships.

THINK LIKE A RECRUITER WHEN BUILDING YOUR RESUME

As mentioned in Chapter 3, most recruiters search for candidates using keywords. Why? Most recruiters are not experts, or even very knowledgeable, in the field that they are recruiting for. Usually, they go by the titles and keywords that have been given to them by hiring managers.

Therefore, when you are writing your resume, try to think like a recruiter. Ask yourself "If I was a recruiter, what would I be looking for in a resume?" Make sure to use the most commonly known term for your job title. Improve SEO by mentioning your job title whenever possible (without being overly repetitive). Insert as many keywords into your resume as you can.

HOW TO MAKE AN IMPRESSION WITH RECRUITERS

Remember when I said that there are incompetent recruiters out there? On the flip side, there are some job seekers who show a callous, aggressive attitude when speaking with recruiters. This approach is a mistake. Recruiters are usually the first gatekeeper you'll interact with, so it is important to make a good impression on them.

So how do you make a good impression when speaking to recruiters? Here are some tips.

1. **Be professional, not casual.** Your conversations with recruiters should be about your work history, not your personal life.

2. **Be positive and upbeat.** Like all people, recruiters like positive, upbeat individuals. Being negative makes you seem disgruntled, which may cause a recruiter to form a negative opinion of you.

3. **Never be aggressive.** Never take an aggressive attitude with a recruiter. It will make that recruiter not want to work with you and you won't move forward as a job candidate. Even how you answer your phone can impact how a recruiter views you. If you answer in a belligerent or abrupt tone, that first impression might cost you an interview.

4. **Do not use slang.** This might sound ridiculous, but I have been called "dude" or "buddy" during my first conversation with some candidates. Needless to say, they didn't get past that first interaction. If your speech is littered with slang words, it's a good

idea to practice speaking in a more professional manner.

5. **Always be honest.** This has been mentioned several times in the book already. Without exception, you must be honest about your background.

6. **Don't be a diva.** No one (and this includes recruiters) likes a person who's temperamental and difficult to please. If you come across as arrogant, you might not move forward in the hiring process.

7. **Don't focus on salary.** For many people, salary is all-important. Salary is important, but limit how much you talk about it. Show more interest in the company and role being presented. If you just focus on salary, the recruiter might think you are only interested in the money and not the role.

HOW TO CONNECT WITH RECRUITERS

Making connections with recruiters is an effective way to expand your job search. Below, you will find ways to connect with recruiters:

1. **Connect with recruiters on LinkedIn.** To do this, go to LinkedIn (*https://www.linkedin.com/*). In the search bar, enter the industry you work in and the word "recruiter" – e.g. "technology recruiter". Profiles of recruiters who specialize in your profession will pop up. To connect with a recruiter, click the *Connect* button next to their picture. After they accept your request, send them an email stating that you are

looking for a job. Almost all recruiters will accept your invite request, and some will respond to your email.

2. **Research agency recruiters in your industry.** One way to do this is by Google search: In the search box, type "recruitment agency" and your desired industry. Once you have a list of agencies to contact, send each one a resume and, if possible, try to connect with them via phone. Not all recruiters will get back to you. Nonetheless, those who do will be able to open doors for you.

3. **Ask your current and former colleagues for recruiter referrals.** A great way to connect with recruiters is to ask current and former colleagues for referrals to good recruiters they have worked with.

4. **Apply for jobs that agencies have posted.** Find agency recruiters by applying for jobs that agencies have posted. If you are qualified for any of the roles presented by the recruiter, there is a good chance they will contact you.

HOW TO DEVELOP LONG-TERM RELATIONSHIPS WITH RECRUITERS

You never know when you might be looking for a job. Therefore, it is recommended that you continually develop long-term relationships with good recruiters. If you do so, they will remember you and you will be higher on their list when they have roles. Following are 7 ways to develop relationships with good recruiters.

1. **Give them referrals.** Recruiters love referrals. If you refer other good candidates, you will get in your recruiter's good books. The only time I would not give a referral is if you are currently competing for the same role.

2. **Like their posts on social media.** An easy way to get in a recruiter's good graces is to like their posts on social media sites like LinkedIn.

3. **If the recruiter does something good for you, send them a thank-you email.** Recruiters are more likely to remember you if you send them a thank you email for something they have done for you. To go one step further, send their manager an email praising the great service you received from the recruiter. Everyone likes someone who is thankful, so a thank you email will go a long way.

4. **Send them email greetings on holidays and birthdays.** A small thing you can do to develop your relationship with a recruiter is to send them a quick holiday email, and if you know their birth date (perhaps it is on their social media profile), send them a quick birthday greeting.

5. **Always be punctual for interviews.** Being responsible, in terms of being on time for interviews, will also make you memorable to recruiters.

6. **Be honest in your dealings with recruiters.** As discussed multiple times in this book, always be honest with recruiters. This includes keeping your word about going to interviews or being honest if you accept a role outside of that recruiter's openings.

7. **Always return recruiters' calls, texts, and emails.**
Even if you are not working, it is highly recommended that you always answer or return recruiters' emails, phone calls, and texts promptly.

CONCLUSION

Connecting and creating long-term relationships with recruiters will help you discover jobs in the hidden job market and increase your chances of landing a job.

16

RESEARCHING COMPANIES

Job boards may not list all open jobs in your field, as some companies' jobs might not be promoted outside of their website. So, it's a good idea to research companies in your chosen industry and directly apply for jobs on their websites.

HOW TO RESEARCH COMPANIES IN YOUR PROFESSION

Researching companies is quite simple. Below are 4 ways to do so.

1. **Research local companies in your profession.** Think of all the companies in your local area, or even outside your area, you would like to work for. Go online and look up their career pages. If any of these companies have job openings that match your qualifications, apply for those jobs using the career page.
2. **Ask current and former colleagues.** Ask your current and former colleagues about companies in your local area

that have open roles in your specialty. Once you have a company's name, look up the company online, find their career page, and see if they have any job openings. If they have openings you like, apply for those roles.

3. **Do a Google search.** You can research companies in your industry by doing a simple Google search. In the Google search bar, enter your local ZIP/postal code and your industry. Companies in your local area will pop up. From the results, choose a few and click on their sites to see if these companies have job openings listed on their career pages. If anything catches your interest, apply.

4. **Research fast-growing companies.** Many small but fast-growing companies may not have the budget for online job ads or recruiters. This being the case, they make a potential area to research. To do this, type "fast-growing companies" in the Google search bar. You will find a list of different sites. Look at this list and if any catch your eye, click on the company's website and see if they have job openings in your skillset. If any positions match your needs, apply.

CONCLUSION

There are many jobs that may not show up on job ads. Therefore, researching companies and applying directly on their websites will give you additional avenues to search and apply for jobs.

17

NETWORKING

Networking is a great avenue to pursue when job hunting. It can help you can find leads that turn into potential jobs.

Networking can take many forms. This chapter will discuss these in detail.

NETWORKING WITH FRIENDS AND FAMILY

An obvious place to network is to ask friends and family if they know of any job leads. Most of your friends and family will be happy to help, so this is a great place to start your networking.

NETWORKING WITH CURRENT AND FORMER COLLEAGUES

The best way to network is to contact current and former colleagues and ask them if they know of any job opportunities. Many will not mind referring you, so it never hurts to ask.

Most companies love external referrals. They are more likely to trust a referral coming from a current employee than a non-referred candidate. In addition, there could be an incentive for an employee to refer you to a job; companies may give employees cash or gift incentives for a successful referral.

NETWORKING WITH PEOPLE IN YOUR INDUSTRY

If you belong to an industry group or association, you might want to contact individual members and/or the association itself to see if they know of any job opportunities.

NETWORKING WITHIN YOUR CULTURAL OR RELIGIOUS GROUP

If you belong to a religious institution or a cultural organization, you can ask members and/or leaders of these institutions if they know of any opportunities. As some of these groups act as an extended family, they might go out of their way to help; they might even send emails to members requesting their help in your job search.

NETWORKING WITH ONLINE GROUPS IN YOUR PROFESSION

Joining online professional groups in LinkedIn and Facebook can be an avenue to network for roles. It never hurts to join several of these groups and post that you are looking for roles.

Don't forget to look for open roles posted by members, too.

BE YOUR OWN RECRUITER

A final form of networking that we'll discuss is directly contacting hiring managers. This the most difficult and time-consuming form of networking, but it's quite effective.

Basically, you become your own recruiter.

To do this, you need to research companies in your local area and find out who the hiring managers and directors are. To find hiring managers, go to LinkedIn and search the company name and the title of the person you want to contact. For example, if you are an accountant, you could type "accounting manager or accounting director Acme Accounting".

Send LinkedIn invites to the people who appear in the search results. If they accept your invitation, InMail or email them, asking if they are looking to fill any roles and letting them know you are looking for a new job opportunity.

Hi Mark,

Thank you for accepting my LinkedIn invite. I am a skilled and certified accountant with 10+ years' experience in your industry. I was wondering if you have any current openings or know of someone who is hiring.

Sincerely,
Jane Smith

Worst-case scenario: The manager will not like that you contacted them directly. But that will be the exception to the rule. The more likely scenario is that a manager will either ignore the email or respond. I know of many job seekers who landed roles by contacting an employer directly. In fact, for my second recruiting job, I directly contacted the manager and was hired.

CONCLUSION

By networking with all your contacts and with any organizations you belong to, you will expand your job search. You'll have a network of individuals looking for jobs for you.

18

HOW TO INTERVIEW
FOR A JOB

You can have a killer resume. You can apply for job after job. But if you do not interview well, you will have a hard time getting hired.

In fact, the most qualified candidate is not necessarily successful; in many cases, the best interviewer gets the role.

During the interview, you have a short time to convince a hiring manager that you are the right fit for the role and the company. As interviewing is such an essential key to success in landing a job, this chapter will teach you how to do it effectively. Having this great foundation will increase your chances of being hired.

THE ART OF INTERVIEWING

Interviewing is a skill. As with any skill, once you understand the rules and practice them, you can become an expert.

What is the art of interviewing? It is being able to sell yourself and your abilities to a potential hiring manager – based on how you answer their questions.

You might think "That sounds easy, but it's actually hard!" Have no fear; interviewing is a skill you can master. I'm going to show you, step by step, how to interview effectively.

KNOW YOUR RESUME, BACKGROUND, AND WORK HISTORY INSIDE AND OUT

The first step to a great interview is to **know your resume inside and out.** That includes dates, titles, specific roles, education, and anything important on your resume. If you do not know your resume well, read it over and over again until all significant facts are memorized.

During most interviews, you will be asked to summarize your background, so you must know your work history inside and out too. Many people think they know this, but when they actually are in an interview they can't recall specifics about their work history or education.

Knowing your background goes beyond the fundamentals of knowing where you worked and what title you held. It includes remembering detailed aspects of your major accomplishments and how you handled situations based on those experiences. In preparing to interview, list all your experiences and accomplishments. Review this list until you've mastered the information.

TELL A SHORT STORY

An important part of interviewing is being able to tell short stories about your experiences.

During an interview, you must make an impression on the interviewer by providing relevant, interesting information about your background. This is where short stories come into play.

Try this exercise: Come up with at least five short stories based on the experiences in your resume. Start by making a list of 20 positive accomplishments you've had in your career. Rank them from the most to least impactful. Then take the top five and think of each situation in detail and how each made a positive impact in your career.

Can't think of any? Use the examples below for inspiration.

1. Winning an award at work and how you achieved it.
2. Completing a major task or project and how you did it.
3. Dealing with a tough client and how you managed that situation.
4. Figuring out a major problem and how you solved it.
5. How you created revenue/went over quota and how you exceeded your goals. (For salespeople)
6. How you dealt with or improved a tough situation, turning it into a good situation.
7. How you were promoted or recognized and how you achieved it.
8. How you built something from scratch, be it a department, a product, or anything of importance.
9. How you achieved high engagement scores, low turnover, or a high-performing team. (For managers)
10. How you saved your company revenue.

Now that you have your five accomplishments and have thought about the details of the events, create a short story in your head for each one. Write the stories down to help you remember them. Make them brief but compelling—this will to paint you in a great light. Practice telling your stories aloud until you know them by heart.

HOW TO ANSWER THE 20 MOST COMMON INTERVIEW QUESTIONS

Interviewers repeatedly ask candidates the same questions, regardless of the industry. If you understand the true meaning of these questions and prepare great answers ahead of time, you will increase your chances of landing a role. Below are tips on answering the 20 most commonly asked interview questions.

1. Why are you looking for a new position?
When answering this question, always speak in positives. If you are currently employed, do not mention that you're looking for a new position because of performance issues, management issues, or other conflicts. If you answer negatively, you will be seen as a liability.

Unless you're interviewing for a sales job, don't say you are looking to make more money. Doing so will make you seem money-driven as opposed to job-driven. A good answer to this question is, "I am looking for growth and advancement opportunities."

2. Have you ever interviewed or worked for our organization before?
If you have interviewed with the organization before, the interviewer will check to see how your previous interviews went. If you have previously worked for that company, your past performance records and hire eligibility will be verified. Therefore, always answer truthfully.

3. What do you know about our organization?
This question checks to see if you have done your

homework and actually know about the organization you are interviewing with. Employers want to see that you are passionate about working for them. In preparing for the interview, research the company. When it comes time to interview, you will be able to recall positive facts about the company and communicate the reasons why you are interested in working for them.

4.   Why do you want to work for this organization?

This is like the previous question; you will need to do your homework beforehand and research the company. Give the employer specific reasons why you want to work for them, based on the research you have done. Positive answers like culture, career growth, advancement, and chances to learn new skills will get you in an employer's good books.

5.   Please go over the work history/education on your resume.

The interviewer is looking to get a basic understanding of your background. Even though the interviewer probably has your resume in front of them, give a basic summarization of your relevant positions and education. Expand on this by providing examples of your major accomplishments and achievements. This is a great opportunity to sell the interviewer on your background, proving that you are a perfect fit for the role.

6.   How many years of experience do you have?

This is not the time to exaggerate. Answer this question honestly. Potential employers can and will find this out in a background check.

7. Why do you feel you are the right person for this job?

The point of this question is to see why you believe you are qualified for the role compared to other applicants. If you do not answer with good, solid examples, it could be game over for your interview. Think of something that will quantifiably convince the hiring manager that you are the right person for the role. For example, a person interviewing for a sales position might answer, "For five years, I have exceeded sales targets for your competitor. I could do the same for this organization."

8. What are your weaknesses? What areas do you need to work on?

In this classic question, the interviewer is trying to gauge your honesty and self-awareness. You should reply in such a way that you do not come across as flawed but you're still giving a concrete answer.

There are several ways to tackle this question. One is to give a weakness not relevant for the job, such as a back-office accountant saying they would like to improve their public speaking. Another way is to show that you are improving, such as, "When I first started, my public speaking needed some work, but through practice, I have made huge strides and now consider myself a decent public speaker. My goal is to become a great public speaker." A third way to answer this question is to put a positive spin on it, such as being a perfectionist.

9. What are your greatest strengths?

The interviewer is trying to see how you could be an asset to their company. Give them a few examples relevant to the role that will sell them on you. An example for a programmer might be, "I have superior analytical skills, which allow me to diagnose issues." If you are a great team player, you might answer, "I'm an expert at interacting and collaborating with large groups." If you're an innovator, you could say, "The ability to create new designs from scratch is my greatest strength."

10. Tell me about an accomplishment you are proud of.

The interviewer is looking to see what differentiates you from other candidates, based on your accomplishments. Mention one or two accomplishments, e.g. performance awards, major projects you have completed, or even outstanding work reviews you have received. Everyone has had some accomplishments at past jobs. If none spring to mind for you, think hard and be creative; you'll find something to be proud of that you can mention in your interview.

11. What was your biggest failure at your last job?

This is a very tough question. The hiring manager wants to see what failures you've had and what you've learned from these mistakes. Answer in a way that puts you in a good light but is honest. For example, an HR professional might mention an over-achievement goal as a failure: "At my previous job, I was only able to get 8 out of 10 policies approved by leadership. However, from this experience, I learned that every leader has different needs, and after applying this lesson I was able to get my next four policies approved."

Think of something similar, based on your own job

experiences, and put the most positive spin you can on your answer.

12. Why is there a gap in your resume?

If you have any gaps in your resume, there is a good chance the hiring manager will ask you about this. This might be the hardest question to answer during an interview. For starters, if you have a valid reason for a gap, such a going on maternity leave or taking care of a sick parent, explain this to the interviewer. If you were laid off for non-performance issues, such as downsizing, you might say, "The gap in my work history is from being laid off as part of a corporate restructuring. It had nothing to do with my performance." If you have references to verify this, give them to the interviewer.

A gap caused by being fired from your last job may be the toughest one to explain. Answer truthfully and tell them that you were terminated. This information can easily be found during a background check, so be honest. If there was no just cause for the termination (such as new management getting rid of the old guard) let the interviewer know this. If you have any references to back this up, you should have them in place for this question. If there was just cause for the termination, be honest about it, but be sure to emphasize what you learned from the experience and how you corrected it. For example, a person might say, "Early in my career, I was terminated for not being punctual. But I learned from my mistake and, in the 10 years since, I have never been late." Downplay the termination as much as possible, but be truthful.

13. Tell me about a time you had to work as a team

to accomplish a goal. **How did you work with other people? What was the outcome?**

This question looks at your ability to work in a team. This is not the time to focus on your individual accomplishments. Demonstrate how you cooperate and collaborate with others to accomplish a goal. For example, a payroll analyst might mention having to work with a team of payroll professionals to implement a new payroll system, explaining the part each team member played and how each member's collaboration contributed to the successful completion of the project.

14. Tell me about a time you encountered a challenge at work and how you dealt with it.

Obviously, the interviewer wants to know how well you deal with a challenge. You might answer by recalling a challenge you faced and how you overcame it. Don't leave out the details. An example might be, "At my previous job, I was given five business days to learn a new software system. I put in extra hours, worked with the vendor to get the basics down, and learned how to use that system within the time limit. This challenge taught me that I can learn a complex system quickly and achieve a goal, even with a tight deadline."

15. Tell me about a time you had to deal with an angry internal or external client. What was the scenario? What did you do to turn that relationship around?

This question shows the interviewer how you deal with frustrating situations and how calm you are likely to remain. Make sure to recall a scenario where the way you handled the situation turned an angry client into a loyal, satisfied one. For example, a marketing professional might say, "I was given an internal client who was not happy with their past dealings with the marketing department. I reestablished the relationship by meeting with the client and listening to their needs. After identifying what they were looking for, I could then deliver exactly what my client wanted. The client was ecstatic and is now one of my biggest supporters."

16. What are your short-term and long-term career objectives?

A company wants to make sure that the person they hire will stick around. This question is a way for an interviewer to see if you are looking to stay in the role (or not) and to see what your long-term ambitions are.

When answering about your short term goals, make it clear that the role you are interviewing for meets your short-term goal, and give examples of why it does.

For your long-term goal, tell the interviewer you see yourself still in the company but in a more advanced role. Mention a specific, realistic role that you see yourself working in.

17. How many weeks' notice do you need to give your current employer before starting a new role?

This simple question checks to see how long it will take before you can start working. Most employers want people to start right away.

18. Where are you in your job search?

This question checks to see if you are interviewing anywhere else and at what stage. Keep your cards close to your chest and tell the interviewer that you are interviewing for roles but this is the one that most interests you. This will make them feel you are committed to moving forward with the role.

19. What is your current salary, including the full package? What is your salary expectation, including the full package?

This is one of the most difficult questions to answer because you need to be upfront about your salary and benefit needs. At the same time, you don't want to put yourself out of the running by demanding a salary that is too high.

One way to go about answering this question is to ask them what salary they offer for someone with your experience. If they answer, go with that if it meets your expectations. You can also say you are looking for a fair salary package based on your experience.

If you are forced into giving a number without being given any numbers in return, try to name a realistic salary. If asked about your current salary and benefits, be honest; this can be found out in the background check.

Note: In some places, it is illegal to ask about a candidate's current salary.

20. Do you have any questions for us?

How you answer this question is crucial because it shows your interest in the role. Don't say that you don't have any questions. Think of intelligent, insightful questions that will make a lasting impression on the hiring manager. For example: What do you expect the person you hire to accomplish in 3 months? 1 year? 3 years? What do you like about working for this organization?

THE 4 PS IN INTERVIEWING

They say there is nothing like a first impression. In fact, many hiring managers will make a decision about your candidacy in under a minute. Within that first minute, be it on the phone or in person, if you do not create a positive impression, the rest of your interview is over.

The interviewing process actually starts during your initial interaction with recruiters or hiring managers. In all interactions with hiring managers and recruiters, whether through email or phone, always think of the 4 Ps: Polite, Professional, Prompt, and Positive.

Polite – Always be polite in your interactions with hiring managers. Never be rude, abrupt, or disrespectful in any way. Over the years I've interviewed and interacted with candidates, there have been many who didn't move forward because of being rude, abrupt, or disrespectful.

Politeness starts even before you say hello. You can show it in how you pick up the phone. When answering your phone, always have in the back of your mind that a hiring manager or recruiter may be calling; your tone should be respectful, never cold or abrupt.

Professional – In the business world, there are unwritten rules of professionalism when interviewing. The most important thing to remember is: Don't use slang, and don't speak to potential decision-makers in a casual manner. For example, you should never call a hiring manager dude, man, or sweetie. Also, do not use words that are not common in mainstream speech.

Prompt – Not being prompt in your emails, not returning phone calls, and showing up late to interviews are basically death sentences to your chances of landing a role. If you delay returning phone calls or emails by even a day, hiring managers may move on to other candidates. Being late for interviews by even a few minutes will communicate that you are not serious about the job. For in-person interviews, I recommend leaving your house early to ensure that you arrive on time.

Positive –In general, people like those who are positive and don't want to be around those who are negative. Keep this in mind when you interact with decision-makers. Never talk negatively about past roles, bosses, or anything else. Hiring managers want to find people who are a pleasure to be around (as opposed to a miserable curmudgeon).

HOW TO ANSWER A QUESTION ABOUT SOMETHING YOU DO NOT KNOW

During an interview, you will be asked a question to which you do not know the answer. Always be honest and admit that you don't know. But reply in a way that shows confidence.

For example, a hiring manager might ask if you have experience with a piece of software that you have never used.

You could answer by saying, "I'm an expert with ABC software, which is very similar, so it won't be a problem picking this one up." To an interviewer, this answer might even sound better than someone who actually knows how to use the software but appears uncertain, answering, "I am okay with it."

If you don't know the answer to a question, you can say you are a quick learner. Give the interviewer an example of a time when you learned a skill quickly. The hiring manager will see that, even though you might not have the experience they're looking for, it's something that you should easily be able to learn.

DON'T RAMBLE ON

In an interview, your answers should be interesting and impactful. Even more important, they must be concise and on target. Do not ramble on and on.

Many people, including hiring managers, have short attention spans and do not have the patience for long-winded answers. By talking too much, you will lose your audience. That might cost you the job.

BELIEVE IN YOURSELF

In order for a potential employer to believe in you, you must intrinsically believe in yourself. You don't ever want a hiring manager to feel any doubts about you. If you exude doubt, fear, and trepidation when you are interviewing, you will appear incompetent.

If you get very nervous or are filled with self-doubt when

interviewing, you must learn to change these thought patterns. Earlier in my career, I used to also fall into this pattern of being nervous during interviews. My nervousness was in large part due to being very self-conscious—I naturally talked fast, slurred my words, and spoke with a thick northern-Canadian accent.

How did I change? Instead of focusing on my faults, I started to focus on my strengths. I began to intrinsically believe that any job I would go for, I would get. And guess what? My nervousness vanished, I aced my interviews, and job offers came pouring in.

What is the point of looking at your faults when everyone has strengths? Try this exercise: Write down all your job-related strengths and accomplishments. Read this list over and over until you start to realize—and believe in—all the tremendous things you can do.

Does this exercise work? It worked extremely well for me. Now, almost any job I interview for -- despite the fact that I still slur my words, still talk fast, and still have a thick northern-Canadian accent -- I get. Why? My self-confidence convinces the hiring manager that I am the right fit for the role. I believe in myself, so they believe in me too.

HOW TO DO A PHONE INTERVIEW

There can be times in the interview process when you will be asked to do a phone interview. Phone interviews are like in-person interviews except, in most cases, you do not see each other face to face. Below are some tips on how to interview over the phone.

- Take the phone interview seriously. Treat it like a regular in-person interview.

- Always be punctual.
- Since there are no facial clues in a phone interview, speak in a positive tone and exude an upbeat vibe.
- Try not to sound robotic when speaking. Let your personality come through.
- Smile. Your smile will be heard in your voice.
- Never chew gum or eat during a phone interview.
- Go to a quiet place where you will not be disturbed.
- Speak slowly and pronounce your words clearly.
- If you use a cell or cordless phone, make sure the battery is charged and it has a good signal.
- Make sure the phone you use allows you to be heard and you can hear the interviewer.

PRACTICE MAKES PERFECT

Think of an interview as a play. Can you imagine an actor not practicing his lines before a play? He would mess up or completely forget his part and the play would be a disaster.

My recommendation is to practice interviewing over and over with someone you trust. Practice answering the 20 questions listed in this chapter. Practice the five short stories based on your business experience. During your practice interviews, have your "interviewer" ask you random questions that you are not prepared for. This will help you think on your feet and become used to the unexpected.

By taking the time to practice interviewing, you will be very comfortable answering questions during a real interview.

INTERVIEWING ODDS AND ENDS

How to Dress - Always wear business attire unless you are told otherwise or if you're in a profession where more casual clothing is worn. Generally speaking, men should wear a dark suit and tie with nice dress shoes and women should wear a professional suit with nice dress shoes. If you're a woman and you wear heels, wear small ones. Both women and men should limit jewelry and dress conservatively. In either case, I personally recommend going the whole nine yards and wearing the nicest, most expensive clothes you can afford to give a good first impression. If you don't have business attire and can't buy a new interviewing outfit at this time, there are some charitable organizations that provide dress clothes for individuals who cannot afford them.

Handshake – Always give a firm handshake but do not squeeze too hard. Always shake with your right hand, even if you are left-handed.

Making Eye Contact – Always make proper eye contact with those who are interviewing you. Do not look down at the floor or into space.

Remember to Smile – To reinforce your positive vibe, remember to smile at everyone.

No strong perfumes or colognes – Although it's important to smell good, you also don't want to overwhelm your interviewer with strong perfumes or colognes.

Do not interrupt the interviewer – It is considered rude to interrupt an interviewer, so don't do it.

Do not chew gum – Chewing gum or eating food during an interview is not good manners. Wait until the interview is over to pop anything in your mouth or have a snack.

CONCLUSION

Interviewing is the final step in landing a role. It is vitally important that you learn how to master this skill. By following the guidelines set out in this chapter, you will learn the fundamentals of interviewing, which will help you make a good impression on hiring managers. This will give you an advantage over other candidates.

19

THE JOB OFFER

After going through all the hard work of creating a resume, searching for a job, and interviewing, you can still blow a job opportunity at the offer stage. This chapter will show you what to do – and what not to do – when accepting or negotiating a job offer.

DON'T DELAY ACCEPTING AN OFFER YOU LIKE

As soon as you get an offer you like, you should accept it without delay. Do not play hard to get. If you play games at this stage, an employer might withdraw the offer.

MAKE SURE YOUR REFERENCES ARE READY

At the interview stage, you should already have references prepared and ready to give to whoever asks for them. When choosing who to list as a reference, always pick people you trust to give a great reference. If possible, have backup references, just in case some of your references can't be reached. I would recommend having at least five references, including three managers and two colleagues. Remember, it is not acceptable to use close friends and family as references.

When you send a potential employer your references, let the people you've mentioned know so that they're expecting to be contacted. Also, give them a friendly reminder to complete their references quickly. Some employers will cancel an offer if the references are not completed right away.

ACCEPT THE FIRST GOOD OFFER YOU RECEIVE

After getting an offer, some job seekers may wait to see if a better offer comes along. In my opinion, this is a big mistake. You should always take the first good offer that comes your way. If you don't have other offers on the table but you still hold off accepting one you do have, you could lose that first offer. The employer may move on to other candidates if you wait too long.

WHAT IF THE OFFER ISN'T WHAT YOU EXPECTED?

If the offer is slightly less than what you wanted but you can live with it, you should accept it. If the offer includes other perks (such as a flexible schedule or career advancement) that make up for the money you won't be getting, you also might consider accepting it.

If the offer is below your expectations and there are no other incentives, consider negotiating. In your negotiation, politely let the person making the offer know that you mentioned your salary expectations during the interview process and that's what you need to accept a job offer. In some cases, the employer will meet you in the middle. They may even accede and give you the salary you desire.

LONG-TERM JOB STRATEGIES

Even after you get hired, you should never stop having a long-term job strategy. In today's economy, there are very few jobs that you keep for life. That being the case, you should always keep your resume and LinkedIn profile updated and stay in touch with recruiters. Even if you are looking for promotions internally, make sure your information is always up to date.

CONCLUSION

By following the suggestions in this chapter, you will be able to determine when to accept a job offer and how to handle negotiations. You also understand the importance of having a long-term job strategy.

20

WHAT IF YOU HAVE BEEN UNEMPLOYED FOR A WHILE?

Losing a job is a tough situation for anyone to go through.

Being unemployed for a long time can even be tougher on the psyche. The longer a person is out of work, the more financial worries and other hardships they have. And the longer a person is jobless, the less interest employers will have in them.

The goal of this chapter is to give you hope that there is a solution to being unemployed. The tips will help you to get back on your feet, even if you've been out of work for a while.

BELIEVE IN YOURSELF AGAIN

As I mentioned in Chapter 1, it is important to move from feeling sorry for yourself to a more positive mindset. Start to believe in yourself again.

Put a stop to the negative thoughts about what happened in the past. All these thoughts will do is prevent you from moving on with your job search and with your life. In fact, if you continue to be bitter about your employment situation, employers will pick up on this. The cycle will continue.

Today is a new day. You have valuable skills to offer. Believe that you can change your situation. Adopting this positive outlook will put you one step closer to your new job.

MODIFY YOUR RESUME AND LINKEDIN PROFILE

If you've been out of work for an extended period, you should modify your resume and LinkedIn profile to fill in those unemployment gaps. Here are some useful tips.

1. **Remove months from your work history.** To make it appear that you have not been out of work as long as you have, remove months from your work history dates. See the following work history example of a receptionist who worked from December 2015 to February 2018.

   Receptionist, ABC Corp   2015-2018

   This makes it look like she worked at her last job longer without lying about the dates.

2. **Include a justifiable reason why you have been out of work.** If you have a good reason for being out of work, such as taking care of a sick parent or coming off a maternity leave, list that as the most recent job in your resume to justify your being out of work. The example would look like the one below.

   Sabbatical to Care for Sick Parent   (2018 – Present)

   Some hiring managers will be understanding about a situation like this and move forward with the candidacy; there is a justifiable reason why you were out of work for a long period.

3. **Include a current, relevant part-time job.** If you have worked even a few hours in your field, you should mention that on your resume. You do not have to mention it was even a few hours. For an example, look below.

   Receptionist (Part-Time), ABC Corp (2018 – Present)

4. **List relevant volunteer or academic work as your current job.** If you have done any relevant volunteer work or academic work in your field, you may put that as your current job. An example of this is found below.

   Receptionist (Volunteer), ABC Corp   (2017 – Present)

VOLUNTEER IN YOUR FIELD

To get back into the job market, you might consider volunteering in your field. For some, this might seem like a step back, but for those who are stuck, not moving forward in their job search, this could be a good solution.

By working hard at your volunteer role, the company you volunteer for may see you as an asset. Even if the company does not hire you, they may be willing to recommend you for other jobs. Or you may meet coworkers or managers who are willing to be used as references.

Volunteering can help land you a job because it fills gaps in your resume and keeps your skills sharp. Below you will find ways to find volunteer roles.

1. **Look at volunteer job sites**, such as:
   https://www.idealist.org
   https://www.volunteermatch.org/

2. **Research leaders in your profession.** To find volunteer roles, contact leaders at places you would want to work, including directors and HR managers. Write, phone, or email them, briefly explaining your desire to volunteer for their organization. To find leaders, go on LinkedIn and enter the company and the title of the person you want to contact in the search box. For example, if you are a contact center rep, you might type "Acme Company contact center manager and director". Send LinkedIn invites to the people appearing in the search results. If they accept your invitation to connect, send them an InMail and tell them that you would like to volunteer. Below is a sample InMail:

Hi Jane,

Thank you for accepting my LinkedIn invite. I am an experienced contact center professional and I am looking to volunteer as a contact center rep. Who in your organization may I speak with about volunteering?

Sincerely,
Michael Smith

WHEN TO CHANGE YOUR JOB FOCUS

There might come a time when you need to consider switching your job focus.

Unfortunately, as the economy changes, some careers die out. Skills can become obsolete. Sometimes all search avenues have been exhausted and there are no jobs in your profession to be found in your area. In these situations, you might have to retrain and move on to a new career.

Some countries have job transition programs that help cover the cost of retraining for those who are changing professions.

HOW TO FIGHT AGEISM

An unfortunate aspect of society is that, in some cases, seasoned workers are discriminated against. Below are two strategies to combat ageism in the job market.

1. **Remove education dates.** The date someone graduated college or high school can indicate their age, so taking those dates out of your resume can make you appear younger. Here's how to list education without dates on a resume:

    EDUCATION

    Bachelor of Commerce - University of Texas

    At some point, you still might have to give education dates, such as the reference stage, but by then it will not matter. The employer will already be interested in you as a candidate.

2. **Take years off your resume.** You might consider hiding a long work history to avoid age discrimination. If your previous job history is not relevant, don't list it. If you are ever asked, you can say you left irrelevant jobs off your work history. If you have a job history that is dated yet relevant, you can create an "Other Work Experience" section in your resume. This is where you list your previous roles but not the dates

worked. That section might look like this:

OTHER WORK EXPERIENCE

Nurse Manager – Health Hospital

Nurse - Health Hospital

Patient Care Tech - Health Hospital

CONCLUSION

Being unemployed for a long stretch of time can be hard on your psyche. By using the strategies in this chapter, you can get energized for your job search and find your next job.

21

GETTING A JOB AS A NEW GRAD

If you were to ask people which job was the hardest for them to get, they would most likely say it was the first job in their field. This is because, in many cases, you need experience to get a job. This chapter will give new grads great tips on how to land that first job.

GIVE THE IMPRESSION THAT YOU HAVE MORE EXPERIENCE THAN YOU DO

Landing your first role in your profession can be quite competitive. Many new grads are competing for very few spots. To make yourself stand out from the competition, your resume should give the impression that you have more experience than you do. Here are three suggestions on how to do that.

1. **Include volunteer job-related experience.** If you have any volunteer unpaid experience in your field, you should make sure you list that experience. See the following

example.

Data Analyst (Volunteer), ABC Corp   2017
As a volunteer data analyst, I assisted the strategy department in determining the effectiveness of major projects' outcomes. Used Excel and Salesforce to attract data to analyze success.

2. **Include job experience not related to your field.** When looking to land your first job in your chosen field, you can list unrelated work experience on your resume if you don't have any relevant work experience. This will show potential employers that you have experience in a work environment. In addition, many employers value unrelated experience, such as working in fast-food or retail, because it develops your work ethic and customer service skills.

3. **Include academic job-related experience.** If you have no job-related experience but have academic-related experience, elaborate about that in your resume. See the example below.

Academic Project – J2EE Mobile Banking Application
University of Waterloo   2017
For my final academic project at the University of Waterloo, I designed and developed a mobile banking application using J2EE, Java, Spring, Struts, ibatis, JSP, AJAX, HTML, Oracle 12g, Maven, Log4J, SLF4J, iText, EditPlus, Eclipse IDE, JUnit, WinCVS, Axis2, JSON, and UNIX.

HIGHLIGHT ACADEMIC ACHIEVEMENTS

While academic achievements are always important to include in a resume, highlighting them is even more crucial when you are looking for your first job. Any academic achievement you have obtained, such as a high GPA, scholarships, awards, or any other accomplishments, should be listed on your resume.

FOCUS ON ENTRY-LEVEL JOBS

As a new grad with little experience, you should focus on looking for entry-level jobs. These are jobs where employers want to hire someone who has little or no experience.

Starting with an entry-level search might seem like common sense, but a lot of grads don't make applying for entry-level jobs their focus. Most want to jump right into a high-paying job with all the perks and benefits. But they forget one thing: those jobs require experience.

Experience is something a new grad doesn't have. By putting in the time and working in an entry-level position, you'll gain the experience that employers are looking for. Once you've done that, you'll be qualified for more advanced roles.

You can look for entry-level jobs on all major job sites, specialty sites, aggregators, job classifieds, and entry-level job sites.

GET EXPERIENCE BY INTERNSHIPS OR VOLUNTEERING

If you do not have any job-related experience, a great way to get it is to do an internship or volunteer in your field.

Many companies offer both paid and unpaid internships designed to help those breaking into that profession gain experience. If an intern performs well in their role, a company often will hire them when the internship is finished.

To find internships or volunteer roles, look at all major job sites, specialty sites, aggregators, job classifieds, entry-level job sites, and internship/volunteer sites.

PROPER INTERVIEWING ETIQUETTE

You worked hard in school, got good grades, and completed an internship. But, when it comes time to interview, you mess up. This is very common for new grads – and it can be corrected.

Knowing how to interview is the number-one thing entry-level job seekers have trouble. Most new grads do not know how to communicate in the corporate workplace. When they interview, they express themselves too casually and litter their speech with slang. This turns potential employers off. My advice to new grads is to practice proper interviewing etiquette and learn to speak in a professional manner.

To improve your interviewing skills, please refer to Chapter 18.

CONCLUSION

Getting that first job in the profession they trained for can be difficult for new grads. Applying the tips in this chapter will make getting your first job easier.

CONCLUSION

For many individuals, looking for a job can be one of the most stressful times in their lives.

This does not have to be the case for you. In this book, you have learned how to build a stellar resume and LinkedIn profile, how to find the best jobs, and how to effectively interview. This solid foundation will help you move forward and be successful in your job search.

Thank you for reading my book, and I wish you the best of luck in finding your next job. If you enjoyed this book, please give it a review on Amazon.

WOULD YOU LIKE AN EDGE IN YOUR JOB SEARCH?

My company, Elite Pro Resume Service, can help you land your dream job.

As you know from reading this book, I strongly believe in helping candidates prepare for a successful job search. I devote the same level of excellence to my clients, providing each one with industry-leading support, personal service, a flawless and professionally edited resume, and a 100% satisfaction guarantee. The following services are available to job seekers:

- A one-on-one intake session geared to customizing your resume. No template resumes here!
- Resume keyword optimization, which increases your chances of standing out on hiring managers' search lists.
- Assistance creating impactful LinkedIn profiles, cover letters, executive profiles, and thank you letters.
- Interview training and preparation.
- Job search training.

For more information, visit *https://www.eliteproresume.com/* or contact me directly at *steven@eliteproresume.com.*

ABOUT THE AUTHOR

Steven Mostyn, MBA, is a leading expert in resume writing, job hunting, and recruiting. He's also the CEO of Elite Pro Resume Services. A three-time bestselling author, he has written for Forbes, HR.com, ERE Media, and others.

For over 20 years, his custom-crafted resumes have helped thousands of clients, from CEOs to new grads, successfully land jobs at Amazon, Marriott, Microsoft, IBM, Wal-Mart, and many other dynamic organizations.

As a recruiter, Steven has helped some of North America's largest companies – including Oracle, Deloitte, Aon, TD, and AdventHealth – find qualified staff. This experience allows him to understand what kind of resumes and cover letters resonate with hiring managers and recruiters.

Steven has a bachelor's degree from York University and an MBA with a focus in HR from Centenary University. He's also earned recruitment and HR certifications from Seneca College, HireVue, and LinkedIn.

Follow Steven on social media or contact him via email or his website.

steven@eliteproresume.com
https://www.eliteproresume.com/
https://www.linkedin.com/in/stevenmostyn
https://www.facebook.com/eliteproresume/
https://twitter.com/top_headhunter

OTHER BOOKS BY STEVEN MOSTYN

Recruiting 101: The Fundamentals of Being a Great Recruiter
https://www.amazon.com/Recruiting-101-Fundamentals-Being-Recruiter/dp/0991490029/

Job Search: Fundamentals of Effective Job Hunting, Resumes, and Interviews
https://www.amazon.com/Job-Search-Fundamentals-Effective-Interviews/dp/0991490037/

If you enjoyed this book,
please kindly give it a review on Amazon.

CPSIA information can be obtained
at www.ICGtesting.com
Printed in the USA
LVHW112114280323
742714LV00004B/572

9 780991 490004